Slaying
the Marriage Dragons

SLAYING THE MARRIAGE DRAGONS

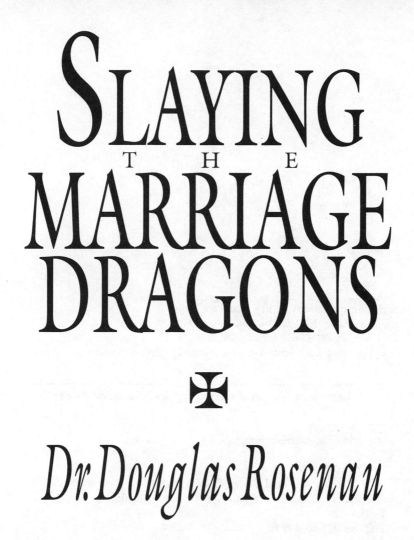

✠

Dr. Douglas Rosenau

VICTOR BOOKS®

A DIVISION OF SCRIPTURE PRESS PUBLICATIONS INC.
USA CANADA ENGLAND

Scripture quotations in this book are from
the *Holy Bible, New International Version,*
© 1973, 1978, 1984, International Bible
Society. Used by permission of Zondervan Bible Publishers.

Library of Congress Cataloging-in-Publication Data

Rosenau, Douglas.
    Slaying the marriage dragons / Douglas Rosenau.
        p.   cm.
    ISBN 0-89693-851-4
    1. Marriage – United States. 2. Marriage – Religious aspects –
Christianity. 3. Communication in marriage – United States.
I. Title
HQ734.R7S68 1991
306.85–dc20   91-19907
                                                                                    CIP

1   2   3   4   5   6   7   8   9   10   Printing/Year   95   94   93   92   91

Contents

Dedication

To my wife
Catherine

This book is a tribute to her support and love —
she has helped me slay some dragons
and has taught me so much about
intimate companionship.

The Marriage Dragons

I hate seeing people miserable and lonely. In my office I daily struggle with the heartache of couples whose marriages are deteriorating. This is especially troubling when intimate companionship is right at their fingertips.

This book grew out of my alarm over the many marriage problems that were needlessly choking out a happy, supportive friendship. I realized that couples keep repeating the same mistakes over and over again. These recurring intimacy killers are the marriage dragons—the top five most devastating saboteurs of God's wonderful gift of intimate companionship.

BUSYNESS. No couple is immune to this modern plague. Busyness crowds out time to be lovers and friends, leaving mates exhausted, separated, and unhappy.

LITTLE NEGLECTS. An accumulation of small neglects, not major traumas, devastatingly choke out loving companionship. Love can be destroyed by neglecting to confront little problems, to affirm and continue small loving gestures, and to overlook unimportant flaws.

AFFAIRS. In over fifty percent of the Christian couples I counsel, one or both partners have committed adultery. Few behaviors can so completely poison the specialness of marital intimacy.

PASSIVE HUSBANDS AND ANGRY WIVES. Poor communication creates a vicious cycle of anger, disappointed expectations, hurt feelings, and attack or withdrawal. Sluggish husbands who are ignorant of relational skills cause desperation in their wives.

CODEPENDENCY. Each mate brings into marriage a backpack of ineffective ways of interacting with others. This personal craziness creates destructive marital patterns. Intimate companionship is short-circuited; it takes two whole people to make a whole marriage.

The first five chapters of the book will describe these dragons that threaten the marriage of a typical couple. The first step in preventing a problem is to truly understand it.

CHAPTER ONE

Busyness
Erodes Companionship

✠

*A*lex and Jenny sat in my office, harassed and exhausted. My heart went out to them as I empathized with the pain and confusion mirrored in their faces. On the phone their presenting problems had been concern over dwindling sexual activity, the fear that they were no longer best friends, and a level of stress in Alex's life that was causing an ulcer. Jenny was worried because sexual intimacy had usually been a good indicator of the condition of the rest of their companionship. They had not had any activity now for four months.

Alex looked at me and said in a pleading and discouraged tone, "I hope you can help us. Jenny and I put off getting counseling because we were too busy. I hope it isn't too late. We realize our counselor will have to work under three tremendous handicaps. We don't have enough time, or energy, or money."

As I let this sink in, I thought sadly that they were not an unusual couple. Waking up on the run and scurrying from hasty meals to carpools, to work, to home chores, to sleep, and then right back at it. Then I remembered this was the third night in a row I was going to be working until after 9 P.M. I suddenly did not feel very immune.

Alex and Jennifer were an average middle-class couple. He was thirty-nine and had a demanding but fulfilling job in the training department of a communications company. He often thought how lucky he was to be using his natural aptitudes in a career he enjoyed. She was a full-time homemaker and mother of Todd who was twelve and Melissa who was ten. Alex and Jenny had been married seventeen years. Both were committed Christians and truly enjoyed their mutual faith and church involvement.

There had been some rough times in the marriage and they had not always felt in love, but had somehow remained good friends. As they remembered the first year or two of the marriage with its financial difficulties and some shattered expectations, they were grateful that a close companionship slowly emerged. Each started to feel the other was truly a partner in this marital venture. The commitment kept deepening and the creative love somehow broke through the dark clouds of their rough times.

Now, Alex and Jenny tearfully related how desperately they missed being intimate companions. Like Adam and Eve they had learned to be physically and emotionally naked without any shame or hesitation. This sense of being soul mates was slipping away. As they explained what they had built in their marriage and did not want to lose, it seemed a beautiful definition of what marital friendship is all about.

They warmly shared amusing and tragic moments as they lovingly created a mutual history and new traditions. They eagerly stored up events when apart to communicate in the time they carved out each day for each other. Both felt they were better people for being in the marriage. They supported each other's goals and lovingly rubbed off rough edges. Neither felt dominated but enjoyed a healthy interdependence. The spiritual sharing in the relationship was very bonding, and they regularly prayed together at night.

Alex felt good about the progress he made in getting beyond the scars of his dad dying when he was ten. He became more demonstrative and both greatly improved their conflict and communication skills. Jenny struggled with accepting her own sexuality and letting go of her extreme need for control, and made dramatic improvements in this area of their relationship. Now, she can relax and enjoy her sexual feelings.

These skills and their mutual nurturing were special to each of them. As they saw their companionship deteriorating, Alex and Jenny were scared. They didn't want to lose what they had worked so hard to gain. They were bewildered that this was happening, in spite of feeling extremely blessed in the areas of careers, faith, and family.

TYRANNY OF THE URGENT

● FAMILY. Alex and Jenny had both wanted children but waited almost five years before having Todd. As they think back, they are reminded what joy and revolutionary changes his birth brought into their lives. Though friends tried to tell them, no one adequately described the fatigue and pressing demands of an infant. And then there was that feeling of panic and excitement when Melissa came along. They soon realized that one child plus one child equaled four times the amount of energy and time required.

I asked Jenny what a typical day was like, and she said that this Thursday of our therapy session was pretty normal. I think it would help you to capture some of the fatigue and stress of busyness if you would hold your breath while you rapidly read the rest of this paragraph: get up and take a quick bath, read the Bible and meditate, get kids up and going, fix breakfast, help Alex match tie and shirt, carpool Todd and Melissa, make beds and do household chores, come to therapy, help prepare church senior citizen's luncheon, quick grocery shopping, Melissa to swim practice, pick Todd up and fix snack, meet with friend Lois who is going through divorce, prepare supper, go to handbell practice at church, get the children quieted down, do load of laundry, hug Alex and beg off once again from fatigue and awkwardness (he laughed in our session in a helpless but understanding manner), go to sleep.

It did not take a genius to make the diagnosis: Too Busy! Some major sabotage of companionship was taking place and there were no simple solutions. Alex and Jenny wouldn't trade anything for the love and purpose that the children brought into their lives. They often thought of college and grandchildren and how neat it would be to have Todd and Melissa dropping in and out of their home over the coming years. They often discussed possible ways they could streamline their lifestyle, but somehow there was always an emergency or an urgent task to be attended to around the kids.

Their second honeymoon was abandoned because of Melissa's appendectomy, and the remodeled bath and Jacuzzi were eaten up by two years of braces for both the children. The leisurely walks after supper were short-circuited two evenings a week by music lessons. They worried about trying to be superparents, and yet they did want to develop the children's potential and provide opportunities they didn't have in growing up. When Jenny observed other children, she didn't think she and Alex were doing any more than their neighbors around them.

What a roller coaster of emotions! They felt proud in fulfilling the parental role well and seeing their children grow up contented and well-rounded. They also felt extremely frustrated and resented the demands and the toll the children were taking on their marital companionship and their private time alone.

This was further complicated by having both sets of parents within easy driving distance. It was great having available baby-sitting, and both appreciated having the joy of a close family support network. The problems centered around the guilt of not seeing family often enough and trying to fit their parents' needs into an already full schedule.

For example, the triple by-pass surgery on Alex's stepdad two years ago created such extra stress and emotional drain that it took three months for Alex and Jenny to recuperate. Trying to balance a Christmas vacation away to relax while also spending time at both parents' homes got to be quite an exhausting feat. Yesterday, Jenny's mom called and said she would be in the neighborhood and could they do lunch together today. Jenny hated to put her off, but lunch with today's schedule was impossible. Jenny promised they would drop by on Sunday afternoon for a visit, and they could see her mom's new upholstery on the sofa then.

Jennifer felt undersupported at times as she struggled as the homemaker to organize schedules and juggle time, money, and energy to keep everyone happy. Fights sometimes ensued with Alex asserting that he was trying to be a good provider and get them out of debt. He was not sure how much more he had to give. He tried for awhile to take more responsibility with the children but never seemed to follow through. Though Jenny didn't think he understood, he did realize how much their parents and children encroached— their couple time alone together was almost nonexistent. They also knew the importance of private time to exercise, do hobbies, and recreate. This too was infringed upon by rushing around attending to urgent matters, while the most important priorities were being neglected.

• FAITH AND MINISTRY. This frenzied pace was exacerbated by their Christian faith and gifts for ministry. Jennifer had a special talent for music and the ability to organize/administrate. Alex loved to teach and was able to synthesize material and present it in a practical, insightful manner. His current lessons were on stewardship; but the biblical principle, to those who have much will more be given, was being played out in an unfortunate way in their church and spiritual lives.

Jenny was director of the handbell choir and a member of the church trio. This meant special performances at Christmas and Easter and the usual six to eight weeks of practice beforehand. Alex led a men's breakfast prayer group and co-taught the adult Sunday School class on Christian Growth, as well as serving as a deacon.

Countless times both tried to pull back out of exhaustion and did well at saying no to new commitments for several months in a row. Then a job would come along that needed doing and nobody else was available. It also looked challenging. After a time of prayerful and anguished soul-searching, they would agree to accept another responsibility, but only until someone could be found to take over. Right! With the job well-covered, there didn't seem to be a need for a replacement.

There were no simple answers. Alex and Jenny struggled with fatigue and burnout, but also received much spiritual nourishment and affirmation from their church involvements. They found it exhilarating to use their God-given talents and hoped the stress and exhaustion was a by-product that the Lord could ease. Yet, they were fully aware how their church activities trespassed on their alone time both as a couple and individually. They also knew how desperately their batteries needed recharging.

● CAREERS. The rat race did not end with children and church obligations, for *careers* needed to be factored into their stress equation. Jennifer did not aspire to be supermom, but she considered homemaking an art. She felt frustrated when the various facets of meals, family time, children's needs, domestic chores, decorating, etc. were not all attended to in her own perfectionistic manner. A maid once a week and grandparents nearby helped but the organizing and labor could still get overwhelming, with lists made on top of lists. There never seemed to be a break in the schedule.

Alex knew he was fortunate to have a job he truly enjoyed, but he had given up on ever limiting it to forty hours a week. He got irritated when Jenny complained about needing more time and energy from him — he was not sure where he could find another minute in the day. Alex had come to resent not having time for himself or to enjoy their relationship.

He never thought he would be so tired that he would turn down Jenny's sexual advances. He has though, not even having the strength for pleasure. His position as communications director was tremendously fulfilling, and the money was great, but it did not leave much left over for anything else.

Alex also felt overwhelmed that as he made more money, they still had trouble making ends meet. Neither he nor Jenny were impulse buyers, but they never seemed to have any money left over for savings. This put greater pressure on him to produce and didn't help the busyness-bind. He worked more but couldn't seem to get ahead.

It was hard for him to turn his mind away from work even after he got home. Sometimes in the middle of supper or some other family activity, he would catch himself mulling over a problem from work and completely losing touch with what was going on around him. Jenny got upset with this; but other times, when he tried leaving work at the office, she would complain that he excluded her from that whole area of his life.

Alex and Jenny both knew that the hectic pace of their lives was a bittersweet dilemma. Neither one wanted to change their career paths, but many days they felt completely out of control.

ERODING COMPANIONSHIP

With fatigue and discouragement, Alex and Jenny painfully stated that some of the strengths which they thought would provide sufficient glue for their marriage were weakening. They were frightened by the runaway train of their lives that was taking a severe toll on many important bonds in their relationship.

● SPIRITUAL POVERTY. Their personal and shared faith was always a strong connecting point. Now they felt like the Psalmist David and cried out to God, "Restore the joy of my salvation." Spiritual poverty had crept in and they rarely felt a real sense of peace and joy anymore. Sometimes each of them recaptured some fervor and inspiration with music or teaching, but it didn't last. Their faith had become dry and more of a perfunctory duty than anything else. They didn't look forward to praying together anymore and worship had become routine.

This spiritual poverty was invading all aspects of their lives and relationships. Alex shared that he had noticed a couple of the red flags indicating that he was spiritually running on empty. He quit self-disclosing at his prayer breakfast and avoided the intimacy and accountability. He did not make time for Scripture reading and meditation and was procrastinating in all areas of his life. He was less disciplined at work and at home. Jenny found herself isolating from some of her close friends and leaving immediately after handbell practice. She also was much more short-tempered with Alex and the kids.

● DISTANCING. They also noticed that they didn't enjoy each other's companionship as much. Warm, shared experiences were becoming rare. Even when they went out, it just was not much fun. They did not save up all the little things that happened during the day to share as they used to. There seemed to be no good time to do that, or the tension was so high, or they were just too tired. They would sit across from each other at the restaurant and the conversational and emotional connecting would lag. The intimate "one fleshness" was fading.

Alex loved Jenny's childlike enthusiasm, the way she could get excited about little pleasures, and squeal like a schoolgirl.

She was so fond of his laughter which would spontaneously explode from deep within, and the dimples that showed when his face lit up with a smile. But the laughter and playfulness that both relied on over the years to brighten up the friendship, and give needed relief and perspective, were harder to come by these days.

They used to be lovers and great companions but somehow that has changed for them. The walks, the talks, the comfortable togetherness before going to sleep at night was vanishing. Usually Jenny went to bed and was already asleep before Alex came up from watching the late news. Being best friends was a glue they thought would be good for the long haul in their marriage. Now they couldn't take it for granted. Both spent time thinking over the disintegration of their camaraderie and how they could prevent it from further unraveling.

• LACK OF BOUNDARIES AND PRIORITIES. Alex and Jenny realized that they had neglected some of the important parts of intimacy that protect and nurture companionship. They had not set good boundaries to keep their time alone together a real priority. Both had given each other the leftovers of their energy, making it difficult to creatively feel love and warmth for the other. They didn't disclose anymore, and avoided conflict rather than dealing with it. Children, church, and career had taken control.

Jenny was especially troubled by the loss of sex and saw this as symbolic of the general deterioration of their relationship. Alex explained that at first it was primarily the busyness and fatigue — they neglected to structure in quality time for sex. Now it was awkward and their irritability and resentments got in the way. Their rare feeble attempts always fell short. They both had begun to nitpick about flaws like Alex's weight and Jenny's breast size. This never bothered them before. It was as if a barrier was erected when they did not guard their quality time together. Now they couldn't seem to break through it and so they became more and more distant.

• A VICIOUS CYCLE. Sexual intimacy was always a relaxing release as well as a warm way to affirm love and renew their special, loving companionship. It was a way to temporarily shut out the mean, cold world and nurture each other. Now, they were in a vicious cycle. In their hectic pace, they so desperately needed this sexual nurturing and connection, but the same hectic pace prevented this from happening, and everything grew worse.

They felt so much confusion and pain, and they both cried as they told their story and sobbed that they didn't think they could summon the energy to take the necessary steps to save the marriage. They were so tired and it was beginning to seem hopeless. What started out with so much promise had been harassed to death by the tyranny of urgent tasks.

The stress and emotional confusion was taking a toll on their bodies as well as their marriage. Alex feared he was developing an ulcer and Jenny had constant headaches. Both would have colds for two or three weeks at a time with their resistance always down. Their bodies were telling them to slow down and set better priorities. Both, of course, worked right through their sicknesses, because there was no time to be sick. Fortunately an ulcer could not be ignored like the flu or a cold and Alex's body was forcing him to reevaluate.

Their dilemma was exacerbated by a multitude of important and worthwhile commitments. Where was the place to start setting limits? Jenny's music? The children's amusements? Alex's work demands? Nothing would be easy! The fatigue level made the craziness seem insurmountable. Because of a host of resentments, each was reluctant to be the first to reach out and reinstate some loving, nurturing gesture toward the other. Alex and Jenny concurred with relief that they had not forgotten their communication and companionship skills. They were just rusty or buried under the busyness avalanche.

PLAN OF ACTION

In creating a plan of action, we all agreed that things could not stay as they were. Either there would be serious changes or a divorce was imminent, or even a physical collapse. We also reiterated that there were no easy solutions, but that in coming sessions we would begin the problem-solving. They would need to think through their expectations and priorities and set realistic goals. We would explore together how they might sabotage these goals and how we could covenant together to follow through on them.

Since Alex and Jenny were both willing to acknowledge their personal contributions to the problem, they could start working on their own rough edges and quit whining and blaming. They decided to take control of their lives. They knew it would be difficult, but they were willing to begin letting go of their hurts and resentments. I encouraged them by saying that I would guide them through this growth process. They *could* recapture intimate companionship as they learned to control busyness.

CHAPTER TWO

Little Neglects
Quench Creative Caring

✠

I could see this headline on one of the weekly tabloids: "Swarm of Killer Gnats Overwhelms Unwary Couple!" One husband recently told me, "Eighteen years of little problems are killing us." It hurts to see a major trauma damage a couple's love and companionship. We have all observed the death of a child, an unresolved affair, or bankruptcy rock a marriage. Tragically, more marriages are besieged by little neglects than by major catastrophes. This is sad because it is so preventable.

Many couples fall prey to the Killer Gnats of avoidance, forgetfulness, and nitpicking. Each of these pitfalls is a special type of small neglect. *Avoidance* neglects to confront little problems, negative attitudes, relational ruts until they have grown so large they are quenching love and respect. *Forgetfulness* neglects the small bonding behaviors that help love grow and remain exciting: a flower, breakfast in bed, doing the laundry, being nice when irritable. *Nitpicking* neglects to overlook the unimportant flaws, unintentional slights, minor slip-ups that occur in all companionships. Any intimate relationship can be killed if the mates focus only on the flaws.

When I first saw Bruce and Nancy, they quickly stated they didn't love each other any more. They had been married ten years. They emphasized that their relationship had badly eroded over the past four years and that an important part of it was dead. They still had some commitment to the marriage but even wavered on that at times.

I explained to them I liked the term *creative caring* as a description of love, because it is the creative energy at the core of a companionship. I was not convinced their love, their creative caring, was gone entirely. Most couples fall in and out of the feelings of love over the course of a marriage.

Love melds a couple together in three unique and meaningful ways. It manifests itself sexually in *a playful, exciting bonding.* Companionable love is both *a feeling and a choice,* with laughter, warm sharing, and support. Love is also *a deliberate act of the will* to unconditionally accept and nurture a mate, to be committed to his or her spiritual well-being.

The feelings of companionship and sexual attraction were gone, but Bruce and Nancy's willful choice to be married still seemed to be present. Why were they there in my office if all hope and commitment were gone? Their response to one of my questions surprised me and also increased my hopefulness. I asked them if their marriage had ever functioned well, if they could remember a time when they were truly happy together. They immediately replied, "Yes."

This was a little unusual. Often when couples come for counseling feeling as disconnected as Bruce and Nancy did, their good times are so fogged over that they don't remember them or refuse to acknowledge them. As the story unfolded, Bruce and Nancy still remembered why they had married each other and said that the first four years of their marriage were great. But now they just didn't see any hope; they didn't respect or like each other anymore.

Their hopelessness and discouragement were not that different from what many couples feel. As a marriage counselor, I used to wish for both partners to feel a definite love and commitment. Now I realize many relationships enter therapy with one or both mates skeptical of the marriage surviving, but willing to explore whether it can be revived.

The level of Bruce and Nancy's apathy did arouse my curiosity, since the opposite of creative caring is apathy, not anger or confusion or frustration. Couples who are angry and fighting often remain very connected. Those who don't care anymore will need to work more to rekindle love.

I wondered if some traumatic event had occurred to choke out love and respect. Maybe severe financial problems or codependent scars from their past had invaded their companionship. As we continued to explore their relationship, none of these proved to be accurate. Bruce and Nancy sadly discovered, like so many other couples, that if a marriage is not carefully tended to, it slowly disintegrates under a multitude of little neglects until love is extinguished.

THE GOOD YEARS

Bruce and Nancy had met at a waterskiing party thrown by one of Bruce's friends, and they felt an instant attraction. Though both had dates to the party, they managed to talk some that day. The following week, Bruce got Nancy's phone number and they went out on their first date. They didn't rush it, but the attraction and attachment kept growing. Over the next two months they began dating each other exclusively.

Initially, as with most couples, there was an attraction based mostly on physical and personal appeal. At the party, Nancy had noticed that Bruce laughed a lot; she also loved his hands and hair. Bruce was taken with Nancy's petiteness, great figure, and the way she pitched in and helped, even though she was a guest. The more they dated, the more they found they had in common. They had mutual interests in the outdoors and being active; both loved ethnic restaurants and risking new experiences; they had similar social and academic backgrounds at smaller colleges, and they enjoyed their jobs. Bruce was in sales and Nancy was an office manager.

On a deeper level, they discovered they had common values. Their Christian faith and spirituality was important to each of them. They sought a closer contact with God and grew in their ability to be honest, to forgive, and to love themselves and others. They came from similar family backgrounds. Both dads took time for the children and their moms worked but made homemaking important. Both Bruce and Nancy were careful with money with Bruce being more the penny-pincher.

They were both strong-willed and at times opinionated. Bruce disliked conflict but Nancy pushed him to confront their differences. Just before their engagement, Nancy thought Bruce was too involved with a female colleague. They tried to sort through what was healthy jealousy and what was mistrusting possessiveness. A friend helped Nancy back off a little and encouraged Bruce to realize that boundaries were important and that some of Nancy's jealousy stemmed from truly valuing this partnership and wanting to make sure nothing jeopardized it.

They got married after their initial attraction had grown into a deep love and commitment to each other. During the first four years, marriage just seemed to get better. Oh, there were disagreements and hurt feelings, since each had brought into the relationship some unrealistic ideas of marriage. Bruce thought that the husband should have the major say-so in all financial decisions with a minimum of consultation. Nancy had a good head for business and expected her input to be sought and respected. Buying a new car brought this issue to a head, and they worked through to what seemed a mutual understanding, after much grief and lost sleep.

They grew closer during this time. The birth of their daughter, Heidi, was very bonding. They shared the experience throughout and were awed as they held their baby for the first time. In her second trimester Nancy's sexual desire had increased so that Bruce didn't know if he could keep up. They enjoyed this time and later joked about it. Heidi was very time-demanding. Bruce discovered he could miss sleep easier than Nancy could, and pitched in with early morning feedings.

Bruce remembered his feelings of love and contentment as he watched his wife rock Heidi and softly sing to her. They needed a larger house and both laughed as they recounted how their concerns were more that the mate's needs be met than their own. Bruce had checked out kitchens and junkrooms while Nancy looked at rooms that could be made into an office so some of Bruce's job could be comfortably done out of the home. They felt appreciated, and realized their spouse and lover truly had their best interests in mind.

The third year they were married was tough, with Bruce losing his dad to a heart attack and Nancy suffering a miscarriage. There was so much grief and struggle that neither could always be there to nurture the other. They still clung to each other and entrusted one another with their feelings. They vulnerably cried together, were angry, and prayed a lot after they realized God still truly cared. This was a very bonding time and their creative caring climbed to higher planes and reached into deeper recesses of their hearts and minds.

The only blip on their screen of contentment was Nancy's fear that Bruce did not truly understand how devastating the miscarriage had been. He reacted less intensely and wasn't there to support her. But she didn't think she should bring it up and so let it slide, since she felt his empathy and support in so many other ways. Slowly their wounds healed. Bruce connected with his mother in a new and mutually supportive way. Nancy began checking temperatures and trying to become pregnant again.

INCREASING NEGLECT

The fourth year of their marriage was busy with both getting promotions, the birth of their son, Jason, and Nancy deciding to become a full-time homemaker. There were many adjustments, but they tried to handle them well. The time demands on Nancy were tremendous with two infants, and sometimes Bruce felt neglected, especially when sexual frequency never seemed to pick up even after the episiotomy scars had healed. Bruce tried to be patient and figured things would straighten out in time.

Nancy didn't realize how much she would miss her job as office manager. She ran things at home, and had to organize and make decisions, but it wasn't the same challenge and fulfillment as at work. She especially missed the adult interaction, but she didn't want to complain, because she was the one who had wanted to quit work. Also, Bruce was under a lot of pressure with his promotion to district sales rep.

Nancy missed the autonomy of bringing in her own paycheck and hated to ask Bruce for money. They had a joint account and he reassured her it was *their* money. It brought back some of the negative feelings from earlier in their marriage when she had not felt an equal financial partner. Somehow, buying personal items like clothes and jewelry rankled her if she thought she needed to check with Bruce. It just seemed like his money, no matter what he said.

Jason grew like a weed. She was able to get some breaks from the kids with Mother's Morning Out at her church and Bruce's mom was usually available. But Nancy still felt she was in a rut and her resentment grew. She sometimes thought that Bruce seemed to have more time to worry about his mom than he did to spend nurturing her. She appreciated his mom's help but felt she was also a little interfering.

As Bruce and Nancy sat in my office, they wondered why they let minor problems in that fourth and fifth year of marriage go unaddressed. Now they could see how little issues escalated. One strength of their intimacy had been their commitment to each other and to bettering their skills at communication. Both had tried to not avoid confrontation but assertively disclose what they felt or needed. Bruce knew he feared conflict and had tried to improve. They had used their anger as a signal that something was wrong and needed to be addressed and perhaps corrected. But then they started letting things slide by, maybe out of courtesy or fatigue or avoidance. Irritations began to build, even though the depth and strength of their love still maintained a pretty good relationship. To people in their church, it seemed the ideal marriage.

It wasn't just infrequent sex, Bruce's mom, fatigue, and Nancy's frustration with autonomy and money. Other small fissures began appearing. Over the years they had developed a variety of caring gestures that meant much to each of them. Nancy loved carnations and Bruce would surprise her now and again with a beautiful bouquet. She also felt especially indolent and pampered by breakfast in bed on a black laquered tray they had found for $2 at a flea market. Bruce believed in birthdays and Nancy would fuss over him for a week with cards and little gifts. He also would die for her special meatloaf.

They tried to be loving even when they did not feel like it. Nancy would bite her tongue on a sarcastic retort. Bruce would not forget to compliment and appreciate Nancy even though he was angry or tired. They created many loving traditions and gestures, many caring attitudes and actions that they then began to slowly neglect or forget.

Their spiritual life and Christian faith were vital to both of them. Their love was based upon their Christian principles, and they humbly took responsibility for their actions and often sought the other's forgiveness. They tried to follow 1 Corinthians 13 and lovingly overlook faults and believe and encourage the best in each other. They also knew that they could love each other better if they kept Christ's love and presence centered in their lives. They practiced God's guidelines for a great marriage.

Now, both found their inner wholeness eroding and experienced a deviation from God's economy for loving companionship. Bruce found himself pouting and feeling very misunderstood and unappreciated. Nancy began feeling disconnected from Bruce, with a growing insecurity and a sense of being undersupported. This negative mind-set slowly grew as both experienced increasing resentment and anger. Their marriage started to lose its loving-kindness, honesty, and joyful connecting.

As I listened, I was puzzled. What they were describing somehow still did not account for the terrible state their present relationship was in.

CONSEQUENCES OF NEGLECT

They then began to unfold the last four years of their marriage. In years seven and eight they still connected occasionally and made short-lived attempts to recapture the love and vibrancy they once had. Nancy remembered a relaxing ten-day vacation at the beach. Her folks were at a nearby condo and helped with childcare. By the end of the vacation, she and Bruce were talking more and touching each other with genuine caring. The unresolved issues still hovered in the background, but she could better tune into the reasons she had chosen Bruce and why she respected and loved him.

Bruce too could recall what he now called "token efforts" to reconnect, as the marriage unraveled during the middle years. They would occasionally be very passionate and the effects of a particularly nurturing session of love-making could linger for a week or so. They would tackle a topic and talk for two or three hours. They would share a warm mo-

ment together around Heidi and Jason or go camping for a
weekend. But unfortunately, the overall avoidance and neglect continued.

Then began a period they didn't even like to dig up because of the pain. It was a horror in slow motion. Again
Nancy and Bruce asserted there were no major traumas or
betrayals. The relationship was not adulterated dramatically
with Nancy having an affair. Bruce did not abandon the
family and stay at work till all hours of the night and weekends. The little neglected areas seemed to create a constant
negative mind-set.

In the first years of their marriage, their creative caring was
so positive that little hurts were forgiven and soon forgotten,
small faults ignored, and it was easy to keep perspective.
Now, the opposite was happening, as the mounting neglects
produced endless hurts and disrespect.

Bruce and Nancy knew the irritation and unhappiness
were gathering momentum until they could see nothing positive and focused only on the warts in the relationship. Nancy
picked about his sloppiness, his careless driving, his occasional weekend work, his forgetting to call the insurance agent,
his mother, his chewing gum, the part in his hair, and his
kissing. Bruce criticized her women's group, her sexual desire, her blue leather belt, her intolerance of his family, her
weight, and her lack of personal meditation. Their obsession
with the negative became a deadly enemy.

Bruce and Nancy tried to convey the terrible nightmare
this created. They seemed to grow angrier and angrier until it
not only destroyed love and respect but turned into a hatred
of the other. Their hearts and stomachs ached with the loss
of love and relating. They were desperately lonely with no
companionship available. The rest of life became a fog as
their wounded marriage became the only focus point of their
minds and feelings. Work and the children faded in their
importance as they stumbled through their daily lives. They
were desperately in need of a life-support system for their
marriage but couldn't connect with any intensive care unit.

Surprisingly, they could still keep a facade to friends at
church. They knew counseling might help, but at first it
seemed such an expensive, desperate measure, and then it

seemed almost too late. They tried a time or two to find a counselor, but argued and sabotaged those attempts to reach out for help. When they woke up in the morning, the black clouds of hurt and anger would descend. Occasionally, one or the other would try to reach out, but they never seemed to be able to coordinate reconciliation attempts. One of them would make an apology, but a pouting or angry retort would start the fight all over again. Nothing was ever resolved or forgotten now. Though in saner moments they could see some of the unimportant issues over which they fought, the relationship became a huge, angry impasse with love being daily destroyed.

Little neglected areas came back to haunt them. There seemed so many of them now: the miscarriage and Nancy's feelings of Bruce not truly understanding, Nancy's need for recognition and inclusion in the financial area of the marriage, Bruce's relationship with his mother and her time demands, Nancy feeling too dependent after becoming full-time homemaker, Bruce's dissatisfaction with their sexual frequency, a mutual loss of respect, and their spiritual poverty. The specific issues lost importance as the painful disintegration of the marital intimacy gathered a life of its own.

Bruce and Nancy both said that the hurt and anger were so great that they just went numb and began avoiding each other almost as a defense mechanism. They evolved a civil coexistence that slowly grew into apathy. Bruce had months before moved into the extra bedroom. There were still a few angry clashes, mostly when Bruce tried to make a tentative effort to reconnect. For Nancy, it was all over.

THE RESOLUTION OF NEGLECT
● FACING THE CONSEQUENCES. I asked if their present relationship was not rather awkward at times. Nancy related that they created a united front around issues pertaining to the children. They still maintained a pretty convincing facade at church or business parties and personal entertaining. Both mourned the loss of the creative caring of their marriage and the enriching companionship that love had energized. An awkwardness would occasionally surface when they would forget and lapse into old intimate behaviors—

those loving gestures were so inappropriate in the present state of the relationship. It was also awkward around their family who could see what was happening and felt terrible, but didn't know what to do about it.

When I asked why they had come for therapy at this time, they gave me two reasons. First, they could see the children were scared and hurting. Jason had begun having temper outbursts. Heidi was doing poorly in school, where previously she had excelled. The second reason was that both Bruce and Nancy missed being loved and having an intimate relationship. They were not sure they wanted to rekindle it with each other, but they could not live with the relationship as it was. Nancy wondered about a divorce and moving on with their lives. Bruce hoped a preliminary separation might help. As Christians this made them both uncomfortable, but there did not seem many alternatives.

I responded that usually I was not in favor of separation. Sometimes it served a purpose to let people have the space to sort and change, but overall seemed ineffective. Usually the work could be done better while living together.

At this point I knew I could simplistically state that perhaps love could be rekindled. Their relationship had worked well in its earlier years. I could also in a judgmental way tell them God hates divorce, and they should hang in there and try to work it out. I felt that would be like telling them to think of a food they despised, and then imagine that God and I were going to make them eat it until they liked it. I did not want to lose the opportunity to help Bruce and Nancy by giving simplistic advice or judgment. They needed encouragement and someone to empathize with them. It would have to be a gentle process and I would have to be their hope for awhile.

They felt they had gone through enough pain and angry hatred to last a lifetime. Why open up all the old wounds? The wet blanket of *neglect* and *negativity* had choked out the love, leaving only apathy. Bruce and Nancy's marriage had turned into a completely intolerable and unpalatable commodity.

Even worse, in their indifference there was no desire to try and make it better. The death of love and respect within intimacy has such tragic results. Their solid marital relationship had slowly been quenched over ten years of neglect. It had now bottomed out and that is where we would have to start.

● REKINDLING HOPE. I started gently and told Nancy I knew she had not come for marriage counseling but rather to try and separate graciously with the least amount of damage to the children. I appreciated the painful experience it had been for them to relive for me some of the horror of the past years. I could see that the love and creative caring essence of their marriage seemed to be gone. Nancy could even name the exact date when she had finally given up on Bruce and their relationship and a more total indifference had settled in.

I asked them if they could suspend the apathy for a few minutes and search back in their memories. Could they help me understand some of the qualities of the relationship and their mate that had attracted them to each other and contributed to a successful marriage. I assured them I was not doing this exercise as a quick fix.

Though not easy, both were able to recount aspects of the other and the marriage that had made it strong initially. Nancy related Bruce's physical appeal with his slender build, beautiful hands, and a smile that lit up his face. He laughed so much and had such a positive approach to life. He wanted to understand and please her. Bruce was a leader in a comforting, nurturing sense, both spiritually and relationally. They could talk and, for a man, Bruce has done remarkably well with sharing his feelings. He could get truly excited or cry, and he had learned to express his anger.

Bruce recalled Nancy's self-motivation in tackling even the unpleasant tasks and her childlike enthusiasm about little things in life; she was a warm and efficient mother for Heidi and Jason. Though their closeness had now degenerated, Bruce could remember the excited, curious, and uninhibited sexual partner Nancy was—how once they made love ten days in a row. Both ended the reminiscing by saying how hard it was to tune into the past because it seemed they were talking about a couple they had never known.

I then said that an investment of ten years deserved a few

months of evaluation before totaling the marriage and moving on. I would hate two years from now for either of two things to happen: for them to continue rocking along in the terrible marriage that now existed, or for them to look back and think they might have worked through their problems, and that they had needlessly forfeited something valuable. I would not try to play games; of course, I wished the marriage could be salvaged, but I could see how devastatingly their love had been eclipsed. They obviously had had something good at one time; it was worth a final evaluation and effort.

If they would be willing to invest the time, energy, and money, we would slowly see if love could be rekindled. If not, then we would hang it up. The key ingredient at this point would be reopening their lives up to God's love and help.

I saw Bruce and Nancy wince when I made this statement. They had prayed and nothing had happened. Now they did not trust God and feared He would force them into being martyrs in an untenable situation. I tried to reassure them this was not true. The marriage they presently had was so far from His ideal that He would never want to preserve that. Could they try to trust Him again and let Him breathe forgiveness, change, love, and hope into their relationship? Maybe together He could give us wisdom to try smarter, not harder.

Bruce and Nancy agreed to give it six months. Each was individually going to visit their pastor for a time of confession and soul-searching. Their homework was to stay in separate bedrooms and live separate lives, but go back to courting behaviors: one formal date this weekend doing something each would enjoy, and every day one genuine compliment/affirmation of the other as a person.

The process was for them to start connecting and building anew, while at the same time beginning to release the past. Their discomfort would probably get worse before it got better, as apathy gave way to pain and anger and then moved on to healing. There were no guarantees, and we were a long way away from creative, energizing caring and companionship, or sexual connecting.

They were willing to try and to make some mental choices to love, trusting God to bless and bring the feelings of creative caring back. Avoidance, forgetfulness, and nitpicking were banned from their relationship.

Nancy was skeptical and reluctant, but I told her that was fine. She and Bruce had to be honest this time around. We would not engage in neglect, but love. All misgivings and feelings were worthy of discussion.

CHAPTER THREE

Affairs
Destroy Commitment

*L*et's pretend you have just been assigned to a committee which has been given the task: Find the most effective means for breaking down marriage commitment, for destroying the covenant, "Till death do us part." If the committee searched and brainstormed for weeks, it could not come up with a better means than adultery.

Commitment and adultery are opposing processes. In their very essence, they are enemies. Commitment protects intimate companionship; it draws boundaries and maintains a special exclusiveness. In the marital commitment, mates make continual choices to preserve the integrity of their relationship. Adultery contaminates by adding a foreign substance. *Adulterate* means to water down and destroy exclusiveness.

There are many ways to commit adultery, to contaminate a successful companionship. A couple can allow television, outside interests, financial worries, or children to encroach on their commitment to each other. Moms aren't always aware how they break down trust by allowing the children's demands to make them undependable in meeting their husband's needs. Men do not see how they are damaging the committed exclusiveness by pursuing sports or work demands.

The focus of this chapter is on that especially destructive kind of adultery: the extramarital affair. So often I have sat in my office in frustrated anger and wept over another potentially great marriage that has been mortally wounded by this enemy. Adultery so tragically destroys some of the key ingredients of great companionship: honesty, trust, playfulness, sexual intimacy. Even undiscovered or emotional affairs can take quite a toll.

Although sex plays an important role, affairs are often much more than sexual curiosity and lust. Mates are blindsided by a caring friendship or the need for an ego-boost. Midlife crises make people very vulnerable.

In retrospect, March 16 was a pivotal day in the life and marriage of Norman Jennings. At 3 P.M., he was sitting in the computer lab mulling over his lunch conversation with his friend Bob, the basketball coach and history teacher at their local high school. Norm thought he knew his friend pretty well, but was shocked when Bob told him he was feeling terrible guilt and anxiety over an affair he was having with one of the school secretaries. It wasn't just that Bob was having an extramarital relationship, but that it had been going on for almost a year and he had said nothing. In this fit of honesty, Bob also revealed that this was the third affair he had had in his ten years of marriage.

Norm considered himself fairly worldly wise. Yet, he knew that at twenty-nine, and living the somewhat sheltered existence of a high school math and computer science teacher, there was much he had not been exposed to. He just had not been confronted this close up with blatant adultery, and especially by a close friend whom he thought he knew inside out.

Bob stated that his first affairs were brief encounters more for the thrill of the chase, curiosity, an ego-boost, and illicit sexual excitement. He knew they took some toll on his commitment and companionship with his wife, Jill, but the marriage survived in seemingly good fashion. He felt some guilt over the dishonesty, but was able to rationalize quite easily. He decided that what Jill didn't know would not hurt her. Bob sometimes wondered if he had a character defect that made him pursue other women.

The problem with his present adultery was that it had grown from an enjoyable friendship and there was more emotional attachment involved. He felt in love with Betty and the sex and openness seemed more special than with Jill. He was extremely confused and guilt-ridden. Bob did not want to hurt or lose either his wife or his girlfriend. He was surprised how much Betty had replaced Jill in his love and companionship.

Jill had found out about Betty through some indiscreet phone messages. She had suspected for a while and had been going through agony. She did not want to lose Bob because she loved him very much. After confronting him with the affair, he admitted it but still vacillated between her and Betty. It was a terrible mess and Jill felt angry, desperate, and afraid.

With the help of her pastor and a close friend, Jill retained her dignity and self-worth. She knew she couldn't make Bob do anything. She simply told him she could not live with the present situation. She knew she was a good mate and that they had the potential for a great marriage. He would have to make a choice.

This was the point at which Bob shared all with Norm. He was so distraught that he had been sleeping poorly for months and felt depressed. The more he thought about it, the more he knew he did not want to lose his marriage. Norm felt sorry, even though he knew the mess was of Bob's own making. He strongly encouraged Bob to end the affair and save his marriage. They spent the rest of the lunch planning how this could be accomplished. There seemed no graceful way but to stop his friendship with Betty cold turkey.

THE EVOLUTION OF ADULTERY

● BREAKING DOWN BOUNDARIES. Norm Jennings was a Christian husband who had been married four years and had a one-year-old daughter, Stephanie. He loved his wife and considered himself a married-type person who valued the enjoyment of intimate companionship. If you had asked him if he thought adultery was wrong and destructive, he would have quickly responded, "Yes!" He certainly did not want Sandi cheating on him. Yet, somehow, that afternoon he could not get Bob and his revelation off his mind. Norm had fantasized about the same secretary and now his imagination took off as he thought of her and Bob together. He began wondering and thinking about how it would be to make love to someone new and even pondered whether affairs were always bad.

He arrived home that night feeling very sexually aroused, and he and Sandi made love passionately after Stephanie was put to bed. In the following months, Norm was not completely aware of how much his conversation with Bob had affected him. It set in motion an idea that would begin to snowball downhill, gaining momentum rapidly.

Bob had ended his affair and was trying to make his marriage work. The most important event that had transpired was confessing all his secrets to Jill and truly recommitting to work on the marriage. It was rocky but they were slowly, through counseling, rebuilding. He grieved over the loss of the intimacy and sex in the affair but, like apples versus oranges, he was creating something new and special with Jill. He shared all this with Norm with a profound sense of relief and rejoicing at being out from under the guilt and stress. This time he was going to really change and make good this second chance. He better understood now how much his affairs actually had impacted his companionship with his wife. He was working on complete honesty and setting better boundaries in his thought-life and his behaviors.

All that Bob said seemed to go in one ear and out the other, as Norm became increasingly preoccupied with his own sexual curiosity and his fascination with other women. He began seeing them as sexual objects for affairs or fantasies. He talked briefly with Sandi and asked her if she ever thought about having sex with other men, but the baby cut that conversation short. She did say she had curiosity on occasion, but that it wasn't hard for her to control these impulses. Fidelity created such security for her and an opportunity for a deeper physical intimacy. Norm kept his runaway thought-life secret, not even discussing it with Bob. He rationalized that Bob had enough problems of his own.

He began fantasizing about some of the women at school, in particular Kim, the cute Spanish teacher who was blond, athletic, single, had a great figure, and enjoyed flirting. He daydreamed about the undangerous liaison and what a "safe" affair would be like: It would be discreet and careful with no messy attachments. Sandi would not get hurt because she would never know or even suspect anything. It would be compartmentalized into a guilt-free and passionate part of his life. It would satisfy his need for new and different sexual experiences but be kept separate from his marriage and values.

Everyone would win in this imaginary adultery: Norm would get his curiosity needs met with some excitement added to his life; Sandi would never know but would benefit from a renewed husband who brought some zest back into a stale marriage; and the other woman would enjoy great fun in bed, a little companionship, and the affirmation of being found attractive and desirable. He couldn't even see how crazy and convoluted his thinking had become.

● DISTANCING AND SPIRITUAL POVERTY. It is fascinating in a scary sort of way how the mind can rationalize and move into distorted patterns of thinking that begin to make so much sense. Someone once told me that he didn't think he had completely broken his marital commitment or had been totally dishonest—he had kept his wedding ring on during his affair. In his unchecked desires and curiosity, Norm was starting to inhabit a secret world. At first he was not even aware of the insidiousness of the danger or how his commitment and intimacy were being diluted. He felt he had a right to keep secrets. Sandi was not involved; he hadn't done anything; she wouldn't understand anyway.

Norm now started building a life apart from Sandi. He was not deliberately lying but was not including her in private parts of his existence. He started going to Happy Hour at a nearby pub with other faculty members after school several times a week. Kim and several other women were there, and he felt exhilarated and free of responsibility, mingling with a group that was younger and unmarried. His fantasy life ran free as he imagined what he might do, given a safe opportunity. The laughter and joking became quite suggestive at times, and everyone unwound in a way that Sandi seemed incapable of doing.

Norm's spiritual life deteriorated: church became more of a nuisance and fellowship, self-disclosure, and Christian accountability just didn't fit his busy schedule. His dishonesty was growing, but he was not self-aware enough to see that he was becoming extremely headstrong, guilty, and self-centered. Sandi seemed less appealing, and he was more prickly and insensitive at home. Fidelity had lost its importance and Norm was truly an affair just waiting to happen, with visions of Kim dancing in his head. He was beyond submitting to God's will and way.

● ACTING OUT. July 9 was another momentous day for Norm. It had started off quite routinely — Sandi was away visiting her mom for the weekend so Grandma could spend time with Stephanie. Norm had elected to stay at home and grade papers from the summer school class he was teaching. Sandi's best friend, Alison, called Saturday afternoon and said she was depressed and having more problems with Ken and would it be okay if she came over and talked. Alison and her husband, Ken, often got together with them as a couple, and they had grown quite close over the past two years; earlier in the summer, they had gone to the Bahamas together. Though the vacation had been fun, it was there that Norm and Sandi first learned that Alison and Ken were having serious marital difficulties, especially in their sex life. Norm had spent long hours walking on the beach with both Ken and Alison, listening to their problems, as had Sandi. It had deepened the friendship and Norm felt a warm closeness and empathy for Alison. Over the past few months, he had become important as a male sounding board.

When Alison came over they sat on the couch, and she poured her heart out on how miserable she was and detailed a huge fight they had had the night before. She did not understand Ken's lack of sexual advances and longed just to be held; she felt increasingly unattractive. As her quiet desperation came through, Norm gently took her hand and tried to reassure her that this was just a phase and things would get better. He said he thought her very appealing (he didn't add, "especially in your red bathing suit"), and she should try not to take Ken's lack of attention so personally. He expressed how sorry he was for her pain and that he wished he had better answers.

As he sat in the living room feeling close to Alison and

trying to help her, Norm shared some of his own misery. He related how he was slowly drifting farther apart from Sandi and did not think she understood him. He worked hard to provide but did not feel very respected or nurtured. She had become angry and distant. Last night was terrible as she had firmly turned down his sexual overtures before going away for the weekend, leaving him upset and hurt.

One thing led to another on that quiet Saturday afternoon, the comforting leading into caressing and increasing passion, until Norm and Alison ended up in the guest bedroom. Afterward, fully clothed, they sat once again on the couch in stunned shock and disbelief. Life would never be the same. Both fervently promised that this was a terrible accident and could never happen a second time. They worried together about Sandi and Ken and how this would affect their friendship. They thought the best course of action was to keep it a closely guarded secret.

After Alison left, Norm did nothing the rest of the day. He alternated between extreme guilt to fearful anxiety to sexual excitement, as he reviewed in his mind what had transpired that afternoon. He contemplated how there had been sexual feelings between him and Alison even before this summer. She was so vulnerable and in need of comfort right now. Maybe what happened wasn't all bad. Sandi called that night, and he wondered later if she could hear the guilt in his voice. It was even tougher when he saw her the next day and lived out the week as normally as possible.

Norm and Alison did not keep their promise, with the guilt and fear of hurting their friends and mates being an insufficient deterrent. They arranged a few secret meetings, but mostly they spent time on the phone, as the affair grew in intensity and carelessness over the next four months. Both of their marriages continued to unravel, with their mates vacillating between anger and anxiety, and desperately attempting to keep things from sliding further downhill. All saw the scary specter of divorce looming on the horizon.

FALLOUT FROM ADULTERY

• DISHONESTY AND MISTRUST. In the past, Sandi and Norm had never kept secrets. They had completely trusted each other and had built that trust on rigorous honesty. They had shared openly every facet of their lives and found Ephesians 4 to work as they realized a deep strength in their marriage was putting off falsehood, speaking truthfully, and expressing the truth in love. They had honestly stated their needs and feelings and overall kept the air clear in an open, diplomatic manner.

Though Norm was not at first aware of it, important elements leading up to and during any extramarital affair are secrecy and dishonesty. After his conversation with Bob and his growing preoccupation with himself and adultery, he began building a private world dependent on many little lies both to himself and others. He knew something was happening but could not put a finger on it, so he blamed Sandi. He was unaware that his actions and thought-life were destroying the trust, playfulness, open communication, and sense of partnership. His secret fantasy life and destructive journey into infidelity were excluding her and sending shock waves to the core of the relationship. What they had wasn't special or committed anymore.

It was only with saddened and remorseful hindsight that Norm understood how deeply adultery sabotages the mutual commitment and unity of a marriage. As Christ stated, "A house divided against itself will fall" (Luke 11:17). During this period in their relationship, Sandi and Norm slowly withdrew. The mistrust and lies were taking a toll and their sense of togetherness with mutual goals vanished. Each felt abandoned and angry, grieving over the loss of intimacy. The home was no longer a safe and nurturing place. They both slowly ceased to protect the companionship and the fence of commitment around their marriage.

What Norm had created in his mind as a safe and fun excursion into excitement and ego-boosting became a nightmare. He developed anxiety attacks in the confusion of juggling commitments and a complex web of deceit. After one nerve-racking experience of six different lies in order to gain three hours in a motel room with Alison, he silently lay on the bed and wondered what he had come to. This was indeed like the country song, "third-rate romance, low-rent rendezvous."

He had to honestly admit he missed what he used to have with Sandi. The energy he spent trying to make a liaison with Alison greatly exceeded the reward of their brief and hurried time together. There was the constant, nagging fear of someone coming through the door and the dread of being discovered. He later read a book that stated it so well, "Most affairs seem to involve a little bad sex and a lot of time on the telephone."[1]

• UNRAVELING COMPANIONSHIP. Sandi became confused and angry. Something was seriously wrong. She felt she was missing a piece of the puzzle. She suggested counseling and often cried herself to sleep. She felt so devastated and excluded. She could not connect enough to even discuss how alarmed she was at the unraveling of their relationship. As Norm became more irritable and angrily picked at all the faults in the marriage, she found less and less to enjoy in him.

Fights and nasty confrontations — never, of course, dealing with the real issue — were daily fare in their marriage. Both became painfully aware that love and commitment can be killed in even the best of relationships if it is buffeted enough. In a heartwrenching way, she saw their creative, unconditional love and companionship slipping away. They could not even talk anymore.

A couple of times she suspected an affair, but that just did not fit with her perceptions of Norm and his deeply held Christian values. She remembered the two character traits which initially attracted her to him: his sensitivity and dependable openness. Then a month ago when they were having dinner with Ken and Alison, she looked up and caught an interchange of glances between Norm and Alison that troubled her. She confronted Norm later and he denied anything was going on; she could not believe it of Alison.

Sandi knew that Norm was different recently. He was wearing new cologne; she did not see the credit card bills anymore; there was a lot of unaccounted for time, and he was emotionally always on edge. She especially grieved over the loss of their sexual love. They had had a special recreative playfulness that they both enjoyed. At first, even with their

---

1. Frank Pittman, *Private Lies: Infidelity and the Betrayal of Intimacy.* New York: W.W. Norton & Company, 1989.

problems, they would still make love occasionally, but it was more a desperate coupling than a relaxed togetherness. Now as the relationship deteriorated, sex became secondary and she deeply missed the chemistry and closeness.

When Norm could be objective, he admitted that he missed the sexual aspect of the marriage. In spite of all his fantasized expectations, the affair offered infrequent and very average sex. He was ashamed to admit it—he felt so gullible and taken, and knew now that one woman was not that different physically from another. As Bob had once told him, "Bodies are bodies, and the thrill of the illicit seems to wear off so quickly." He had thought his situation would be different, but now he was seeing more clearly the problems everyone encounters when looking for greener grass.

After listening to so many tales of affairs, I realize that not everyone has Norm's experience. Some, for a variety of reasons, have never or seldom experienced in their marriage the sexual excitement and fulfillment that they have in the affair. This is what happened to Bob. It may be because of the resentment and anger in the marriage and an inability to relax and connect. Affairs also have a magical unreal quality about them. There is the excitement of the illicit and feeling in love.

Norm found the warmth, feelings of being understood, and a sense of being needed that he first experienced with Alison rapidly evaporated under the load of guilt and the energy required for sneaking. Alison was feeling particularly bad about Sandi and their friendship had slacked off. It had become confusion all around. It was probably time to end it, but how? Maybe once again they both needed to agree to stop and this time make it stick; but they had done that several times already.

• DEEPER COMPROMISES. November 20 changed Norm Jennings' life forever. It was the week before Thanksgiving and everyone at school was excited about the coming vacation. Norm dropped by Quincy's Pub, something he hadn't done in a while. The whole gang was there and Kim was in a great mood. As lousy as he had been feeling, he was glad for the release and joined in the T.G.I.F. celebration.

To make a long story short, he ended up sexually involved

with Kim that afternoon. On his way home from Kim's apartment, he did not know what he was capable of next. He had to pull over into a parking lot, he was sobbing so violently. He experienced a renewed terror of losing Sandi forever as it became so clear what a great job he was doing in destroying his marriage and any unique bonding they had had. He was afraid it was irreparable and he cried even more.

HEALING FROM ADULTERY

● CONFESSION AND REPENTANCE. Norm took a detour by his pastor's office and was lucky to find him in. With more healing tears, he haltingly began to reclaim his honesty. He slowly tried to expose all the ugly, secretive and shadowy parts of the past nine months as he went over the decline of his marriage. There was such a relief and release of tension to finally bring everything out into the light of day.

At the conclusion, Pastor Jim prayed with him to help seal the confession and to truly experience God's forgiveness. Norm felt closer to God than he had in a year, but he still could not forgive himself completely. Jim quietly discussed with him what his next options were in facing and dealing with the damage of his adultery. Norm decided that Sandi had been so present in observing and reacting to his deterioration, both relationally and as a person, that the only way to clear the air and begin building anew was to tell all, even the sordid details of Kim. He had to begin to reestablish honesty and trust.

He would inform Alison of what he was doing and end that relationship permanently. Perhaps in the future he would apologize to Ken. While his resolve was still there, he called Sandi from the church office and arranged to have the baby taken to a neighbor's so they could talk without interruptions.

It was easier planned than accomplished. When he got home he forced himself to sit down opposite her at the breakfast table. He started talking, relating all that had happened with as much self-awareness and honesty as he could muster. Norm could see as he was doing this how he was devastating Sandi. She sat in stunned silence at the betrayal and perhaps loss of her husband and her best friend, Alison.

The thought went through Sandi's mind that this must have been something like Jesus felt on the cross. Never before had she experienced such anguish and pain. She thought the past year had been bad, but it was nothing like this. After Norm's disclosure, she did not know what to say and told him she would have to decide what she wanted to do. She began asking a few questions as she tried to verify that this had really happened.

• THE GRIEVING PROCESS. In the following days, she went around in a fog still hoping that somehow she would wake up from this nightmare. She did not know how to handle her feelings toward Alison, who had called and apologized and tried to explain how things had developed. She felt so terrible that Sandi had almost ended up trying to comfort her; then anger took over and she was afraid that the friendship was lost forever. In fact, anger soon became Sandi's dominant emotion.

She put Norm through hundreds of questions as she tried to sort out why this had happened and if she could ever trust him again. Perhaps down deep she needed to see him squirm and to exact some penance. She certainly did not want any more surprises as she learned every nasty secret. She felt so violated and stupid that she had not caught on to what was going on. How could she have been duped and not suspected or discovered the truth sooner?

Sandi's friend Marie turned into a needed sounding board. In their conversations, she was able to vent her feelings and experience some release. In a time of intimate sharing, Marie revealed she had had an affair in the early years of her marriage. It was never revealed and she had worked through to forgiveness and healing. This helped Sandi understand Norm better and how a series of poor choices could be made. Life was not as simple as it used to be. Marie encouraged her to pray for Norm; this seemed to help her anger and resentment.

REBUILDING

The largest question Sandi had was whether she wanted the marriage to be salvaged — her hurt and betrayal were so deep. She thought their counseling was helping, but Norm's sharing of himself so intimately with someone else and his complete disregard for their commitment was hard to accept. She hoped they could rebuild the trust over time. The relationship didn't feel exclusive or special anymore.

Norm walked on eggshells and tried to answer questions and deal with the anger as best as he could. After a while he grew weary of the endless questions and mistrust and wondered if there would ever be healing. Sometimes Sandi woke him up in the middle of the night crying and needing to talk some more. The positive side was that it looked like the marriage was going to be saved. The tough work was slowly paying off; intimate companionship was being rebuilt.

Ken and Alison, Norm learned, were not so fortunate. The affair was the last straw and they were separated, with a divorce in the works. This certainly did not help Norm's guilt, and though he kept praying for forgiveness, the consequences remained very tough to live with.

CHAPTER FOUR

Passive Husbands & Angry Wives Handicap Communication

✠

Several years ago, two teenage boys ran a red light in downtown Atlanta and struck the fender of my car. When the police officer arrived, the young men explained they had never been to Atlanta before. In their small country town, all the traffic lights were hung over the center of the road, never placed on a post on the street corner. They were terribly sorry but they never saw the light. The policeman smiled empathetically and then ticketed them.

Unfortunately, ignorance is not an adequate excuse. The same is true in intimate relationships. While we may understand ignorance and passive lack of involvement, our sympathy does not lessen their destructiveness. Our mate's level of frustration is not lowered because we are not making mistakes maliciously, just ignorantly.

Why are so many married people—and especially the men—handicapped by poor relational skills? Why are so many husbands unable to express their feelings and connect with their wives? The process probably started when they were children and their families modeled ineffective communication techniques—yelled, displayed temper, withdrew from conflict, or defensively debated. Mom and Dad may have been nondemonstrative with their feelings with few hugs or verbal affirmations of love.

Men are not usually socialized well to be intimate companions. They are not taught to value self-disclosure, personal chitchat, or being in touch with and expressing inner feelings. They tend to make sexual interaction more task-oriented (achieving an orgasm) than lovingly communicative and connective. Like the hunters of old, many modern husbands remain private and uninvolved as they pursue bringing the food home. This causes great frustration in their wives.

Many mates get stuck in their own reality and interpretation of a situation and cannot reach out to walk in their partner's moccasins. They have their own language and are unwilling to try to learn to speak their spouse's language. Ignorance of relational skills, like the other marital dragons, often sneaks up on a companionship; later, it is so difficult to overcome the denial and rationalizations. Lisa and Jerry are an excellent example of a typical couple with relational skill deficits — an angry wife with a passive, frustrated husband, and both of them feeling overwhelmed.

I got a message Monday morning that Lisa Wilson had called my office and wanted to ask a few questions before making an appointment to come in for counseling. I thought to myself that she had probably had a major fight over the weekend and was finally desperate enough to seek counseling. Friday evenings and Sunday afternoons are notorious catalysts of conflict.

When I called her back, she wanted to know if it would be at all effective if only one marriage partner came in for therapy. Their relationship was in a bad place, but her husband was very skeptical of counseling and wanted no part of the process. Some frustrated anger then crept into her voice as Lisa strongly stated she didn't care what he thought; Sunday was terrible and they needed help. With fear and hurt, she wondered if she and Jerry were too incompatible to make a good marriage, if too much water had gone under the bridge to ever turn the relationship around.

I reassured Lisa that counseling sounded very appropriate and that even though she felt frustrated and hopeless, I had seen many tough marriages change. I told her the deep hurt and hostility I was sensing needed to be worked through or the marriage indeed would be doomed. With tears in her voice, she asked again if one person could make a difference.

I again reassured her counseling could be helpful.

Sometimes one person can make changes that affect the whole relationship, and then both grow and change. We would have to discuss what she had already tried and what further steps were possible. I concluded by saying that maybe in time her husband would come in if she applied some leverage. This intrigued Lisa, and she laughed when I assured her that this would not include sending Vito out to break Jerry's legs if he didn't come for therapy.

INEPT HUSBANDS AND DESPERATE WIVES

● DISCONNECTEDNESS. When Lisa came into my office she immediately began crying and then apologized, saying she normally wasn't like this. I reassured her that tears were very appropriate and that obviously a lot of frustration and pain had been bottled up for a long time. This sent her into even deeper sobs as she began telling me about Jerry and her marriage. Her husband wasn't able to open up and talk; this left her feeling lonely and very neglected. He worked long hours and did not participate much in the household. They seldom went out alone together and she felt excluded from his life. She had thought men wanted sex, but he would go weeks without initiating any activity.

Emotionally, she was running on empty and felt terribly disconnected. She had almost had an affair with a neighbor who kindly listened to her and actually cared about how she felt. Lisa was glad she had stopped it, but hated being so vulnerable to affection and a listening ear. She had many unmet needs and truly wondered if she had not made a bad mistake in ever getting married. Perhaps Jerry would never change and she was stuck.

As the words came tumbling out, I was glad for the catharsis Lisa was experiencing, but I almost felt like stopping her and completing the story myself. People relating this common condition often think they are all alone and that no one else has experienced these aggravations. Actually, the same story with different players is repeated over and over again.

Lisa hurried to add that Jerry was a good man and father. He worked hard and provided well for her and the children.

He had temper outbursts but had never been physically abusive. She did not want me to think he was an ogre; I probably would like him if I ever met him. But he could not relax and be comfortably demonstrative with physical affection. He kissed and hugged in a tight, tense manner. It was like pulling hen's teeth to get him to sit down quietly and talk about himself, especially his feelings.

She wasn't asking for much: an occasional spontaneous hug, a dinner out and some laughter and chitchat, a phone call here and there, a five-minute sharing of feelings, even a short confrontation. Jerry was so passive in their marriage and she longed for a soulmate. She sometimes cried herself to sleep over their lack of intimacy.

• SEXUAL FRUSTRATION. Lisa especially wished he would hold her and make love tenderly. Jerry settled for a sexual frequency of once or twice a month and even then it wasn't very satisfying. Initially sex had been more passionate, but she got tired of his grabbing her and being so one-track. She wanted romance and sexual touching that was not just foreplay to intercourse. For a while, she did all the initiating, but she grew tired of that too.

She tried to talk through what went wrong with their love life, and I reassured her that her conclusions all seemed plausible. She and Jerry were both fatigued; also, the children interfered. Jerry now feared initiating sex and risking rejection, so he just avoided it; he also seemed to allow her role of mother and longtime wife to detract from her sexiness. I suggested to her that he might experience the close, emotional sex she desired as being too intimate. He also might be feeling very insecure and doubt his ability as a lover.

At first she feared he was gay; then she thought maybe he had a girlfriend; and then she wondered if something were defective with her. The first two she had found to be untrue, but the third she was battling with, since sometimes she felt very unfeminine and unattractive. When she fished for compliments, he would answer with disbelief that she could find herself unattractive. Her worst nightmare was that he might end up like his father: a strong, nondemonstrative man who treated his wife as if she were a moron; he was verbally abusive, neglectful, and very self-centered.

There are often two sexual patterns common to passive husbands. The first is seen in the man who is sexually disconnected. This was Jerry's situation, and it left Lisa at a loss to know what to do with her sexual desires and her longing for closeness. The second pattern is seen in the man who insists on meeting his own sexual needs without concern for his wife's fulfillment. She longs for romance and sexual touching that doesn't have to include intercourse and orgasm. He focuses on activity. Sex is often the only way he allows himself to be intimate and close physically. The wife feels she has no control and gives in just to avoid conflict. Eventually, such hostility builds up that sexual intimacy ceases entirely.

• DESPERATION. Lisa hated herself for thinking this, but she often hoped Jerry would have an affair so she could leave him without the condemnation of her Christian friends and community. Even worse — and she really hated herself for this — she sometimes got so desperate that she hoped he would die and free her from this terrible marriage. I assured her that these were not uncommon feelings, and were indicative of the panic, pain, and desperation she was experiencing.

Lisa wondered if she had married for the wrong reasons and if she had made a bad choice. She felt angry at God and her Christian teachings that allowed a person to make bad choices and then to rectify the mistakes in everything but marriage. In a bad marriage, you had to live miserably the rest of your life. I assured her that was not God's plan. Many of the reasons people marry (wanting to leave home, sexual desire, loneliness) are incomplete and will not last over the long haul. Couples have to continually reaffirm their commitment and build into the marriage worthy reasons that keep them growing together.

I encouraged Lisa to explore whether she and Jerry were incompatible and she had made a bad choice, or whether there were relational and personal skill deficits that could be changed. I asked her what she and Jerry had done so far to make changes in their marriage and whether anything had seemed to help.

She had tried ignoring the problems, hoping they would go away in time. This had not worked; I assured her the head-in-the-sand routine was seldom effective. Lisa had also tried pleading for change and then resorted to angry nagging, neither of which did much good long-term. There would be short-term changes as Jerry resolved to do better, but in a week to two months he would lapse back into the same old patterns of behavior.

She had tried being the submissive wife after reading a Christian book on how to get your husband to change through submissiveness. She thought either she had interpreted the book wrongly or that it was simply bad advice, because nothing changed. If anything, their marriage got worse. She tried to suppress all her own needs and feelings as she built Jerry up and tried to encourage his leadership. She bit her tongue and never nagged or confronted him, trying by her example to win him over and effect changes. The problem was that Jerry seemed to become more self-centered and ignore the problems, thinking everything was better now that she was off his back. She grew angry as all her own needs were neglected and he became less and less accountable.

Lisa stated Jerry probably would recall those "submissive" years as the best in the marriage, but she continued to shrivel up inside, getting angrier and angrier. I told her submission was a mutual and effective Christian concept, but that I did *not* think God's purpose was to use submissiveness to make an inept husband into a model mate. Lisa acknowledged that aspects of submission helped. Things changed as she tried to reach out beyond herself to love Jerry and began treating him with genuine respect. He listened better and felt a little more motivated; but in the long run, submission, as she understood and practiced it, didn't work.

OVERCOMING SKILL DEFICITS

● CONFRONTING. She asked me what I had meant when I said I would help her put some leverage on Jerry. She had tried in the past and it never seemed to work. Were there ways a wife could effectively hold her husband's feet to the fire so he would make needed changes? We both agreed that when it finally came down to it, no person could force another to make changes or come in for therapy. But there were things she could do to create an atmosphere for change, to maintain her own sanity and self-respect, and to maturely confront Jerry's skill deficits. *When* Jerry came in (not *if* he came in), we would go over these ideas further because they were part of the principles of effective communication and confrontation.

Lisa could start by practicing *detached assertiveness.* The detaching part of this process would begin by dealing with and letting go of her hostility and unrealistic expectations. She could then objectively list her nonnegotiables in achieving personal intimacy. With less anger and hurt, Lisa could approach Jerry more effectively and ask for these bottom line needs of intimate companionship, reasonable demands like regular sexual contact (1 Corinthians 7:3-5), physical touching, caring conversations—things she had a right to expect from an intimate companionship.

Assertiveness communicates and negotiates these needs and feelings in a calm, nonaggressive, and yet persistent manner. It sticks to the topic and is based on self-awareness and self-esteem. Assertiveness gets rid of the heat and fog that jam effective communication, and it cuts to the bottom line. I told Lisa that Jerry might feel threatened and interpret her assertive expression of needs as an ultimatum: "You are telling me that if I don't do what you say, then the marriage is over!" I encouraged her not to get sidetracked or resort to angry retorts or threats. She should calmly reply, "I have carefully thought through what God desires in an intimate relationship and I cannot settle for less. I realize this may be something you choose not to do, and that is your right. I'm not sure what that would do to the relationship; we will have to talk about what it means to us if you feel you cannot change with me."

A second important factor in holding Jerry's feet to the fire was to believe that he could change, and that down-deep he would enjoy being her soulmate. The Bible states we all are created in God's image. All mates have feelings, the desire to communicate and a need for intimate connecting. I told Lisa that I helped men change all the time. I think an important dynamic is that I deeply respected and loved them, and challenged them to change—fully expecting they would.

Lisa's homework before our next session was to think

through her nonnegotiables so she could be assertive, not nitpicky. What did she feel she needed in order to meet her intimacy needs? I encouraged her to put these into behavioral terms, not general ideas, specifics like sex twice a week, or ten minutes of conversation every night after supper, or going to bed at the same time.

Lisa expressed how relieved she was to be heard and not get pat answers. She would work on her list; still, she felt doubtful that she could effectively learn detached assertiveness, since her feelings just seemed to bubble up and take over. We took a couple of minutes to practice how she was going to get Jerry into therapy, trying to help her understand the concept of assertive communication. Lisa started with, "Jerry, I know you don't want to go to counseling, but I need this and want you to reconsider. If you don't go, I doubt that the marriage can work." I told Lisa that this was probably better than her previous approaches but still seemed negative and threatening. She tried again, "Jerry, I know you love me and want the marriage to work. It isn't working for me now, but I'm sure it can with the love and intelligence we both have. I need you to come to counseling with me. I think this is a way to acquire the skills to meet each other's needs."

I applauded Lisa's effort as positive, not blaming, but stating her needs and appealing to his logic. This was yet another concept we would have to work on, speaking each other's language and understanding each other's reality and style of relating. Men often need reasons why things will work; yet unfortunately they can be very fragile. She was boosting him with an affirmation of love and commitment, and then appealing to his logic and self-interest that this could be a way to help both be happier. Lisa left feeling more hopeful that a large part of what was wrong in the marriage was ignorance and skill deficiencies. That seemed more remediable than incompatibility or being stuck with a totally defective husband.

She came to the next session a little deflated and described how the intervening week had gone. Her conversation with Jerry about coming in for our next session had actually gone well, and he said he would try to make it. They had made love once and it was better than usual. The problem was a major blowup over his neglect to make vacation plans. Once again, she felt neglected and unimportant; Jerry got defensive and exploded about how he never measured up. He deflected the issue of his forgetfulness into an attack on her, making Lisa the one at fault. Then Lisa blew up and recited six incidents, the last of the six occurring on a cold March day years before, when he had let her down in the same way. From there it got ugly, with neither wanting to communicate but only to hurt the other.

Lisa related that this was a common pattern in their communication, and that it often took weeks to get over the fallout. After last week's session she was even more aware of the killing nature of ineffective relational skills. She felt angry that she had fallen into old behaviors and was perpetuating immature patterns. I reassured her that she and Jerry had no monopoly on techniques for escalating fights and insuring that nothing got resolved: techniques like shifting the blame, withdrawing, attacking, muckraking up old garbage and name-calling. I told her we would go over a list of relational skills the next week when Jerry came in. We spent the rest of the session poking holes in her backpack of resentments, helping her vent her anger and hurts, and then allowing her to let go of them.

I told her that if I had her permission and she would tell Jerry, I would give him a quick call during the week. She agreed. I was afraid Jerry might subsconsciously sabotage the process by being too busy to come in. I know counseling is very scary at first, especially if you already see it as suspect. Lisa did not need another incidence of neglect to put into her steel-trap mind. She was encouraged but still fragile.

The phone call to Jerry went well; I told him that as a marital expert I was concerned about them. I had seen similar marriages end in divorce because of poor communication and a deeply frustrated partner; I appreciated that he was coming in next week and was sure that enough changes could be made to avert a tragedy. After I hung up, I thought to myself that there was nothing like a little scare tactic to insure participation. Often I have to hit men between the eyes with a ball bat to get their attention and effect changes.

● UNDERSTANDING SKILL DEFICITS. Jerry was

personable and concerned about the relationship, as we got started with our session. I asked him what he thought were the strengths and weaknesses in the relationship. He laughed and said he was the main weakness in the relationship, at least according to Lisa. His journey to the point of sitting in my office had not been easy. When he had gotten married, he thought he was very similar to his male counterparts and should make a pretty good husband. He had always been a hard worker, handled money well, and tried to treat people fairly. Then the dissatisfaction had set in with Lisa seemingly always on his back.

At first he tried to shrug it off as "just women" or maybe something to do with PMS. Then he tried to make some changes and talk to her and that went nowhere so he lapsed into avoidance which drove her crazy. The same kind of pattern happened with sex. Now he felt on edge, like he was walking on eggs all the time or going through a mine field, never knowing when one would explode in his face. Jerry said he just didn't understand what she meant by sharing feelings and wasn't sure how the sexual closeness got in such a mess. He felt desire for Lisa, but knew they sure couldn't talk about sex or connect in any intimate way.

As Jerry was talking, I picked up how much of a battering his male ego had taken over the past years. It is not easy to be incompetent in a major area of life, especially if you are male. The strong, silent provider doesn't make a warm, intimate companion; Jerry's lack of skills was deeply frustrating to him, but he wasn't sure how to break through his passive, private shell.

Lisa started crying as we were talking. I asked her what was happening. She said this was the first time she realized Jerry was in as much pain and frustration as she was, just a different kind. I began to encourage Jerry by asking him about his work as a manager and was truly impressed by his skills and abilities. I told him anyone who could do what he does has the intelligence and ability to learn some additional skills in the area of relationships. I gave them a handout with twelve important communication skills (chapter 10), and the three of us went over it together.

I asked Lisa and Jerry which relational skills they needed to work at most. Both thought awhile and then Lisa said she had already been convicted and was even praying about being more detached. She had a lot of hot spots with so much emotional loading. When Jerry hit one of those, she didn't listen or communicate well. She was guilty of letting her expectations and hostility fog up the situation. She could lapse into negative muckraking and hit Jerry with incidents going back to dating days. She was going to have to work hard at backing off and giving him room to make changes.

Jerry's response was not as clear-cut, but he acknowledged he often tried to listen to Lisa while reading the paper or watching a ball game, and that this didn't work. He knew he didn't empathize well, but all this talk about feelings was a foreign language to him. He said Lisa read self-help books, and that when I got into talking about expressing his deeper needs and feelings, I sounded just like her.

I reassured him he had the intelligence and ability to learn about feelings. We could start off by simply looking at three different feelings most people experienced every day: *sad*, *mad*, and *glad*. Which of these was he most comfortable with?

Jerry stated probably *mad*, because he got upset and lost his temper a lot. We discussed how losing your temper may demonstrate that you don't deal with or understand anger well. Anger was his God-given defense mechanism, a signal that something was not right — some need or sense of justice had been violated. He needed to learn the skill to tune into that signal and figure out what was going wrong with him. We would practice on that. One little skill I encouraged was seeing *angry* as a hyphenated word and trying to discover what else was going on: Was he angry-frustrated? Angry-disappointed? Angry-afraid/insecure? I could see this would take some time so I backed off.

I asked Jerry if he was good with *sad* and when was the last time he cried. He said that sad movies made him teary, but he was embarrassed about that. Lisa jumped in and said she wished he would lean on her more and share when he was hurt or sad. I told her this is not the conditioning of men from boyhood on. The messages they receive are: be strong, sissies run for help, quit being a crybaby. Together we all empathized that some of the skill deficits came quite naturally.

Their homework was for Jerry to pick two different emotional topics. In two fifteen-minute sessions he was to try to express his feelings on these topics to Lisa. She was to detach and encourage him to express his feelings as she empathetically fed back to him what she was hearing. She was not to judge or critique. I thanked Jerry for coming and told him I looked forward to working with him and Lisa in the coming months.

● OVERCOMING RELAPSE. The following week when I went out to the waiting room to get Jerry and Lisa for their counseling session, I thought to myself, "We are in for a tough one today!" You could have cut the tension with a knife. Jerry started out by saying that maybe a divorce was inevitable; they had had a fight that began last Thursday, continued through the weekend and still wasn't resolved. Lisa began crying and I quickly replied how gracious God was to give us this fight. We were going to be forced to make deep lasting changes, not try simple Band-Aid solutions.

The story they narrated was just the same old thing: Lisa wanted to go out with Jerry Friday night for an intimate dinner and listen to some music afterward. Jerry was not a late night person and at this point intimate conversation still scared him and he felt inadequate. He also knew that later that night when he was exhausted she would want sex. He reluctantly agreed to go and this hurt Lisa's feelings, so she said to forget it. Jerry gallantly persisted.

Friday night was a bust, with both of them already walking on eggs. Jerry tried not to pout and to engage in chit-chat. During the day, Lisa had gotten her romantic expectations up and was thinking finally they would have an intimate evening together. The talk didn't flow, and Jerry showed his impatience when she wanted to stay for the performers' second set of music. He fell asleep before they could make love. Jerry said his intentions had been good, but he just could not pull it off. He had even determined to initiate sex, but as he held her he fell asleep.

The rest of the weekend degenerated from there into the

same toxic patterns. We took it step by step from Thursday on and discussed what they could have done differently, what skills were missing as each recognized points in the conflict where they could have intervened. Thursday evening Lisa could have empathized with Jerry's fear of long evenings and intimate connecting by setting definite time parameters: "We will be home by 11:30." She also could have verbally expressed her desire for sex at the end of the evening. She stated that would have destroyed the romance. I gently suggested that his spontaneous initiation would come in time. Right now she would remain a very frustrated woman if she expected Jerry to read her mind or break the patterns without some structured guidelines.

Rather than pouting and withdrawing, Jerry could have voiced his concern about the lack of time parameters and his fear of once again not meeting Lisa's expectations. Friday night, if he was tired, he could have held her and told her he would initiate love-making Saturday night, and assured her that she was very special to him. Lisa stated she didn't always need sex. Often she just wanted closeness and a reassurance that she was attractive and he did desire her.

On Saturday, either one could have requested they sit down knee to knee and practice their communication skills. The misunderstanding was pretty heavy, but effective communication has a way of slicing through the fog and reconnecting. Jerry and Lisa were disappointed that the relationship degenerated back to old patterns so quickly and they were unable to kick in their new insights. I assured them that this was common and that I should have warned them. Patterns of eighteen years would not change in a few weeks.

REINFORCING NEW SKILLS

We continued with counseling over the next eighteen months on an intermittent basis. Jerry joined a men's support group and got more involved with men at his church; you would not recognize him today. He still doesn't read self-help books, but he and Lisa have an intimate companionship that is deeply connected. Their sex life took some work, but better relational skills and Jerry's empathy for Lisa and her differing needs helped greatly. He is more confident as a gentle lover and hugger. He recognized what an impact his father made on him and his style of relating. Jerry realizes he will never change his dad, but knows he does not need to copy him. Actually, as Jerry has changed, his dad too has opened up, especially with the grandkids.

Lisa finally feels connected and her intimacy tank is fuller. She discovered Jerry could not meet all of her needs; as she let go of some expectations, she formed a deeper friendship with her best girlfriend, Beth. She doesn't panic as much when Jerry relapses, but talks it out. Both are aware there is professional help available if they hit a true impasse. There are still times she wishes Jerry were more spontaneous and less controlled. She would love it if he could enjoy some more of the things that excite her, like parties and sitting for hours over a romantic dinner. But as she looks around at other couples, she knows she and Jerry have created a solid, intimate relationship. She is thankful for what she has and avoids self-pity or looking for greener grass. Jerry is no longer passive and uninvolved.

CHAPTER FIVE

Codependent Craziness Sabotages Completeness

✠

On the one-year anniversary of her husband's sobriety, a wife gave her husband a bottle of his favorite Scotch whiskey. When later asked about this, she stated, "I am more used to him being drunk than sober; at least then, he needs me." This is a sad but classic example of codependency. Codependent people create crazy, codependent marital systems.

The word *complete* implies that all necessary parts are there and are put together in a harmonious fashion. It takes two complete people to make a whole marriage. The problem is that most of us bring into marriage some codependent traits from our childhood learning and from traumatic events. We are incomplete people and need to be needed. We may feel an imposter and have poor self-esteem — if others really knew us they wouldn't like us. We may have ineffective defense mechanisms and keep our walls up against intimacy. Our lives may be given to melodramatic scenes, but not to making many actual changes.

Unfortunately, when you combine the individual quirks and rough edges of two mates, you produce a rocky marriage with problems that are compounded and difficult to address. Codependency has a way of being hidden by rationalization and blind spots. People don't usually see their own craziness. The impact on intimate companionship can be devastating.

Tom and Laura seemed to bring out the worst in each other.

Their three years of marriage had been increasingly difficult. If they were honest about it, they would have admitted that even their courtship was rocky. Both had shattered expectations early in the relationship and their rough edges kept conflicting.

Laura vividly remembered an incident in their early dating months when she was devastated by Tom's rageful responses to things she did. His angry reactions seemed to come out of nowhere and greatly exceed the insignificant events that provoked them. He always had a need to defensively protect himself. Once she accidentally stepped on his foot and another time was five minutes late meeting him at the shopping center. Both times, his angry response was inappropriate and wrecked her day.

Laura was also frustrated and hurt because Tom could not easily trust her and kept his defensive walls high. She desperately needed gentle touches to feel secure, and a warm sharing of companionship. Tom was uncomfortable with the level of closeness she desired. He expressed affection reluctantly and their most comfortable connecting was through sex.

Tom admitted that he was overwhelmed, as he began spending more time with Laura, by her need for reassurance and constant affirmation of his love for her. She too could be distrusting and put her walls up, but overall had a bottomless need for compliments and support from him: Was she attractive? Would he stick with her? How much did he love her? Could he improve his job somehow? Money was an especially touchy topic, both his lack of it and his spending habits. He acknowledged that he spent unwisely at times and that his job wasn't all that secure. Somehow it just didn't worry him as much as it did her.

CODEPENDENCY AND A CRAZY MARRIAGE

Though the beginning of the relationship indeed had some ups and downs, it was calm compared with what followed. Laura wondered if Tom intentionally put his best foot forward during dating days, even though a few flaws showed, to trap her into a suffocating marriage. Tom thought either that Laura had completely changed or that he was originally blinded by love. Her former insecurities could not account for the angry, hurt, and obsessively unhappy woman she was now becoming.

● SELF-SABOTAGE. They were both caught in a deteriorating pattern of marital conflict. A cycle that neither knew how to break out of was truly bringing out the ugliest qualities in each of them. They both had an idea of what they wanted but they couldn't seem to achieve it. Laura so much wanted security and to feel nurtured and protected in a way that would give her freedom to be herself. Tom needed to feel respected, accepted, and valued, and to have a sense of leadership in the relationship.

They were their own worst enemies. Their childhood scars, ineffective defense mechanisms, and irrational thinking were preventing them from getting what they wanted. Tom had bursts of rage or distancing as he struggled with expressing any of his feelings, especially the hurt or tender ones. He had trouble letting Laura be emotionally close. He tried to change, but had difficulty opening himself up and saying what he was thinking, feeling, or needing. Tom remained a very self-contained, angry, and defensive person.

Laura tried at first to get through calmly and nicely but nothing seemed to work. So she nagged a lot and resorted to stormy crying jags, but they didn't seem very effective either. She knew it was not all Tom's fault. She didn't like the way her insecurity ruled her at times. She was not sure what triggered these overreactions, though she could point to some traumas in her past and believed there was a connection. Her insecurities seemed to center around finances, needing attention, and unexpected events. She could just go to pieces.

Laura also realized she was, at age thirty-one, wading like a porcupine through a pre-midlife crisis. In an irritable and prickly way, she was struggling for autonomy and a sense of identity. She felt as if she had always been bossed by a man, and she was angry at God and men in general, and especially Tom. It's not that she was against marriage, but that she wanted to find herself and was afraid some of her secret ambitions and dreams might slip away forever. She also sadly realized that her insecurity and her inflexible quest for inde-

pendence were effectively defeating some of her needs for
nurturing and protection.

● A VICIOUS CYCLE. A recent Sunday afternoon is a
great illustration of the destructive pattern into which most
of their interactions were degenerating, a vicious cycle in
which Tom was forfeiting the respect he wanted and Laura
sabotaging the security she longed for. Everything started off
with the best of intentions. Tom decided to try to make
amends for the fight the evening before. He knew Laura was
still upset by his temper flare-up when she questioned his
buying season football tickets without consulting her first.

Tom was not sure why he exploded so violently. He
guessed it was because he hated what he regarded as constant
criticism and a lack of respect for his judgment. But he
should have remembered their agreement to discuss any purchase over fifty dollars; he was beginning to acknowledge
that he budgeted very poorly. Once again he messed up a
good thing. That very Saturday morning they had made love
for the first time in ages and had actually felt close for a
change.

So Tom screwed his courage up on Sunday afternoon and
asked Laura to go to a movie that she had been dying to see.
He imagined he would find the psychological dynamics and
romantic story line boring, but he wanted to make up by
reaching out and pleasing her. He did love her and with the
invitation, he even included a partial apology for Saturday
night's outburst.

Ordinarily, Laura would have been surprised and pleased
to go to the movie and would have appreciated Tom reaching out to make amends. But, she had already made plans to
go shopping with a friend that afternoon. She explained this
to Tom who immediately felt very hurt and rejected. Instead
of expressing his hurt and disappointment to Laura, he reacted with his typical anger and told her she enjoyed spending
time with her friend Evie more than she did with him. Maybe she wished she were single like Evie and could run around
with other men. This kicked Laura's anger in and she sarcas-
tically retorted that other men would certainly appreciate
more what she had to offer. The movie and making amends
got totally lost in another bitter fight that ended with Laura

slamming the front door and screeching out of the drive-
way—another melodramatic interchange.

The vicious pattern had struck again, with neither getting
their needs met and both feeling ashamed of their behavior.
After his fury subsided, Tom sat down in the den and pondered once again the dilemma of Laura and their marriage. If
he could have cried, he would have, for the level of pain he
was feeling was intense. He realized this degree of destructiveness could not continue without seriously jeopardizing
their marriage. Not only did he love Laura and feel as close
to her as he ever had to anyone, but he also did not want to
lose his stepdaughter Tiffany.

• PERSONAL INTROSPECTION. Tom knew their
marital difficulties could not all be Laura's fault, though he
blamed her for starting much of it. Lately it was becoming
clearer to him that their compulsive fighting probably had
little to do with the relationship. They each had brought
many scars into the marriage. He knew that his rage predated
Laura and probably went back to childhood hurts and family
experiences.

Recently his pastor encouraged him to read a book on
growing up in a dysfunctional home and to understand the
problems that naturally occur in this type of setting. Their
minister suggested this after Laura confided in him about the
miserable impasse their communication and intimacy had
come to.

Now, alone that Sunday afternoon, Tom slowly remi-
nisced over his childhood. Being the youngest child wasn't
what it was cracked up to be. Dad put in long hours at the
factory and Mom worked hard at the local department store.
Though she did want to take care of him and his two brothers, she just never seemed to have enough energy and tenderness to go around. Jimmy, his middle brother, was always
sick and got more than his share of love and attention. Paul,
the oldest and the athlete, did not seem to care, since he
enjoyed people, achieved success, and got attention from
everyone.

Neither Mom nor Dad were warm, huggy people and seldom gave compliments. Mom seemed to devote most of her
available energy to disciplining, and to taking care of Jimmy.

Dad was hardly ever present, since he worked overtime and often drank himself to sleep at night. Though he did not feel close to Mom, Tom could understand and relate to her better than to Dad, who was truly unpredictable.

Sometimes when Tommy was little, Dad would play with him and be amused by his childish antics. Tom remembered feeling so good about the attention he received and actually pleasing Dad. The very next night he would try the same behaviors, and Dad would get angry and slap him. It hurt so much and was confusing—he was sure that he must be doing something wrong. He didn't know what to expect and shut down his feelings, except for temper outbursts against his brothers and schoolmates. Tom never dared show any anger to Dad, but he could have tantrums with others.

As he grew up, Tommy could somewhat understand why Mom spent more time with Jimmy. He was sick with asthma all the time and became her favorite since she had to give him so much attention. He also realized Mom wanted things to be neat and to run smoothly, which was hard to accomplish with Dad's drinking. Tom tried hard to measure up, but felt he was never quite good enough.

The only person Tom felt totally comfortable around was Aunt Kate, Mom's sister. As he told her some of his secrets, she accepted him and he relaxed. Unfortunately, she lived two states away and their visits were infrequent. As he looked back, he realized that Aunt Kate had a very positive influence on his childhood development.

In high school the girls were interested in him, but Tom felt uncomfortable with the demands of relationships and lived mostly in his isolated world. About the only thing he excelled in was math, but Mom was more concerned about his English grades. He got pleasure by buying—comic books for his collection, junk food, and electronic gadgets. Spending made him feel good. He tried to take care of himself. If he didn't, no one would.

College was not much different than high school until he met Laura. He felt that finally he had someone like Aunt Kate, someone he could truly relate to who would accept him. The problem was that he couldn't get the knack of bringing out the best in a relationship. His outbursts and isolating tendencies upset even Laura. He loved her but couldn't communicate that love effectively.

As Tom sat in his den, thinking over the past with its many hurts and disappointments and emptiness, he knew the time had come for greater understanding and some changes. He would buy the book the pastor had mentioned, and make whatever efforts he needed to. He would persist and learn how to meet Laura's needs and make his marriage whole and fulfilling. He hoped his resolve could last and that there indeed were solutions, as the pastor had suggested.

Laura was once again discussing with Evie her unbearable frustration and the terrible weekend, forgetting she and Tom had made love Saturday morning. Evie, as usual, tried not to give advice but just to listen. As they sat over coffee and a slice of apple pie at Appleby's, Evie asked Laura to do something her own therapist had asked her to do several weeks before: make a list of the pivotal events in her life.

They turned the place mat over and began right there. Evie explained that sometimes people get stuck in crazy patterns that actually are a product of past experiences. Tom helped aggravate what is going on, but there probably was a lot more to it.

A couple of events came to mind instantly. Laura immediately listed getting pregnant at the age of nineteen and marrying Steve, who left her for another woman two years later. The plunge into single parenthood with little support was devastating as she dropped out of college and got a job and struggled to make ends meet. Starting to date Tom within a year seemed a real godsend, since she had quickly grown to hate the jungle of the single dating world. She also wrote down their family move from Ohio to Florida when she was thirteen and the trauma of making new friends. At that time Laura had missed spending time with her dad who became increasingly involved in his job during her high school years.

Laura had to brainstorm with Evie to come up with two or three further pivotal happenings in her life. She listed three weeks of summer camp when she was eight. The feelings of being homesick and lonely were terrible as she wrote tearstained letters home to her mom. She remembered her first sexual experience in high school. She felt like dying when they broke up three months later. She also thought of a couple of happy events: saving and then buying her first car the summer after her senior year in high school; the father-daughter sorority dance her first year of college in which Dad not only came but bought her a beautiful new dress.

Evie then told Laura the second part of the exercise was difficult and might take some professional help. They started together to analyze the events and think what Laura had learned in these experiences, how they had shaped her values and needs, what scars she had received and how they still affected her. Both agreed quickly that men had never been very dependable in Laura's life. Evie wondered if the fairly fresh wounds from Steve and the cruel aftermath weren't especially important in Laura's approach to Tom.

They talked a little while longer and then Evie had to leave. Laura stayed there thinking over a final cup of coffee. She had hated the poverty and struggle after Steve left. She had thought her folks could have come through more, but she didn't ask. She felt all the burden and responsibility of Tiffany—a two-year-old could be very demanding. And then, there were all the feelings of rejection—was Steve's affair somehow her failure as a woman? Had she been too demanding?

CHANGING CRAZINESS

Laura drove home confused about Tom and unsure of what she should do. Their flare-ups were taking longer to get over, with neither one wanting to make the first move or apologize. As she thought over her conversation with Evie, she felt better because she saw some of the pieces of the puzzle were fitting together. She understood more how she and Tom had triggered a lot of insecurity in each other.

● GAINING INSIGHT AND ASSUMING RESPONSI-BILITY. To her surprise, Tom met her at the door, apologized, and said they needed to talk. Somehow she sensed a miracle and said a quick prayer of thanksgiving. This was confirmed later that evening as they sat down and started some of the most honest, humble times of self-disclosure they had ever experienced.

Tom shared his painful review that afternoon of his family

background. Pastor Johnson's encouragement to explore the effects of his childhood was making more and more sense. He could see how his temper outbursts dated way back. They probably began with the inconsistency and lack of nurture in his own family. He had always had to take care of his own interests. Tom admitted it did not all make sense to him, but he loved Laura and was willing to make changes.

Laura talked of her interaction with Evie and making her list of significant events. She too could see how the relationship with Steve and other past experiences were continuing to haunt her. She too was willing to better understand herself and take responsibility for healing the past. Together, they covenanted to get whatever help they needed. Tom was going to call the pastor first thing in the morning and get the title of a couple of good books and make an appointment for them to see him jointly. Pastor Johnson had told Laura of a psychologist who specialized in marriage counseling; maybe they could get his name too.

When I saw them in my office the following Monday, Tom and Laura were still resolved to make changes. They had had another fight that week which confused them some, but they were pleased it had been less in intensity and duration. We began by unfolding the story that has already been detailed. After they had shared with me some of their history, they asked some heartfelt and probing questions. Was the marriage doomed with just too much craziness? Could I help them understand what was making them miserable? Were they perhaps just incompatible? Could changes truly be made and how long would this process take?

● A FOUNDATION FOR CHANGE. I reassured them that change certainly was possible, but that it would take time and energy on their part. There seldom were miracle answers; but as Romans 12 assures us, they could slowly "renew their minds." Looking at the mixture of confusion, hurt, and hope in their faces, I felt a need to encourage them.

I reminded them that they had some of the key ingredients for a successful marriage. They were in a personal relationship with God and humbly wanted His will in their lives and marriage. They were now seeking change and had experienced some eye-opening insights. They were humbly taking responsibility for learning and applying God's truth for relationships. They loved each other and were committed to the marriage. Also, they were in counseling. These factors truly counted for something and would be a basis from which to work. They smiled as they heard this.

Laura admitted that she had a hard time trusting that God had her best interest in mind. Did He just want marriages to work at all cost? I reassured her God was both loving and wise. He knew what they had was a terrible parody of marriage and needed some serious alterations. God, she, Tom, and I all agreed that what they had wasn't working and some major changes would have to take place. The craziness could and would have to be overcome, not adjusted to.

Laura also expressed a fear that she might have to compromise who she truly was and that she would never discover her identity and freedom if she stayed in the marriage. I told her that she and Tom had a sacred trust to be considerate and help each other grow into the best individuals they could be. It would not be an easy quest, but since they were a team, their mutual goal was to help each other develop in a loving and fulfilling way. I suggested they later read together Ephesians 5:28 and 1 Peter 3:7-8.

Tom was fearful that Laura wanted him to become someone he could not, someone far different from who he really was. I reassured him that Laura just wanted him to rub the rough edges off, not change his core being. The craziness he had brought into the marriage — the scars, irrational thoughts, unrealistic expectations, ineffective defense mechanisms (like rage) — was baggage worth discarding. For a few minutes I explained codependency to them.

Tom asked again if they might just be too different to make the marriage work. He mentioned Laura's love of companionship and his introversion as an example of how they were so different. I reminded him that God created every individual with a unique personality, a free will, and a variety of needs and wants. A necessary part of marriage was learning to communicate, confront, and negotiate. Differences provided a richness to a relationship that could strengthen rather than destroy.

• PLAN OF ACTION. Tom was beginning to understand how his alcoholic home had created a great deal of anger and mistrust that spilled over into all his relationships, especially into the intimacy that Laura desired. We would have to explore and resolve the hurt and rage. Laura had known all along that she was scarred by her early marriage, but she had never thought it through very carefully. The year between Steve and Tom was a nightmare. Now she could see why Tom's demands and spending habits really pushed her buttons.

They both were feeling better, so we ended the session. We all knew there was a lot of work ahead, but there seemed more hope because of their clearer self-understanding and their desire to start to make changes. Tom asked how long therapy would last and what would be the plan of action for dealing with their individual and joint craziness. I said there was nothing mysterious about the therapeutic process and reiterated how they were already making tremendous progress. The action plan would focus on several important areas.

In future joint and individual sessions, we would explore family and personal histories more carefully and work through resentments and scars. I would help them learn better communication and relational skills. Together they would support each other in mobilizing an effective support network. Tom wished he had a best friend and I would help him in this. We would also look at spiritual growth and at increasing the flow of loving energy in the marriage. I told Tom that the length of therapy varied but that problems which had taken a long time to develop would take a year or two to correct. We would try to stay sensitive to their time, energy, and budgetary restraints.

Their homework for the next week was to outline a history of their lives. They were to pay special attention to the events they saw as pivotal in developing values, expectations, or scars. The second part of the homework was to decrease the fog in the relationship by loving behaviors. It would be difficult to make changes until the anger and resentment had been lessened. I told Tom and Laura they would not always feel positive, warm, and caring, but that they could choose to treat each other in an empathetic, patient, and nurturing manner. Often if we act loving, we start to feel loving. We closed the session with a prayer for courage and wisdom.

With Tom and Laura and the other couples, we have now explored the five intimacy viruses of *busyness, neglect, adultery, skill deficits,* and *craziness.* The next section of the book will develop a variety of helpful skills and practical solutions to prevent and heal these invaders. We will start with some practical theology and psychology around the principles of confession, repentance, and forgiveness—keys in the maintenance of intimate relationships and the slaying of dragons.

Slaying the Dragons

The marriage dragons create great pain and confusion. In so many destructive ways, they maim intimate companionship. Section Two will explain and teach relational skills that can help couples like Norm and Sandi or Tom and Laura control and heal the damage to their relationships. You might want to think of these skills as processes which need to be incorporated into a healthy. marriage.

These processes are positive actions and attitudes any couple can learn and benefit from. These skills will include effective confrontation, setting goals, building self-esteem, deepening intimate companionship, and practicing better communication techniques, to name a few.

Practice is an important part of any skill-building process. This section provides Time Out *exercises to enable you to truly experience and learn these needed relational skills. Please spend some time with the* Time Out *sections; they can help you to alter your marriage more than any other part of this book, for in them,* you *become involved.*

CHAPTER SIX

God's Plan for Reviving Intimate Companionship

✠

Relationships that have been attacked by dragons often need to be rushed by ambulance to the marriage emergency room where healing procedures can be administered to revive these damaged friendships. Fortunately, there are emergency room techniques for marriages.

God has a special set of skills which mates can practice to revive their short-circuited intimacy. Confrontation, repentance, confession, expression of feelings, forgiveness, and making amends help counteract the effects of sin and emotional damage on intimate companionship. They are God's unique methods for marriage restoration.

Sin has become an important reality for me in my work as a marriage counselor. Our wise, loving Creator designed an effective economy for relationships. Within this economy, for marriages to achieve intimacy they must be committed, honest, kind, disciplined, and forgiving. When couples don't keep within the boundaries of God's economy, they sin.

Each of us knows the painful consequences of bringing destructive attitudes and behaviors (sin) into our companionship. We can empathize with busyness, nitpicking, passiveness, and communication deficits. These sins distance us from God and our mate. The six skills of this chapter address the problems that the sinful marriage killers infuse into our intimate relationships.

• CONFRONTATION shines the spotlight of truth on

the attitudes and behaviors of us and our mates, examining whether they are in accord with God's economy.

• REPENTANCE recognizes and accepts responsibility for our sinful, destructive thoughts and actions, choosing to make necessary changes.

• CONFESSION breaks the secrecy and helps us overcome guilt, allowing for cleansing and increased self-esteem and self-acceptance.

• EXPRESSION OF FEELINGS tunes into anger, grieving, hate, and sadness, encouraging partners to heal and move into acceptance and rebuilding.

• FORGIVENESS lets go of resentment and shame, freeing up emotional energy to deepen intimacy and creative caring.

• MAKING AMENDS restores trust and makes restitution for harmful behaviors, bringing resolution and rebonding into the marriage.

These six skills are very important to a couple. One wife was able to remember them by an amusing scenario she created. She had a terrible boss. She imagined that one day he *confronted* her wrongly for a supposed mistake, then painfully *acknowledged* he had goofed maximally. He crawled to her on his knees and humbly *confessed* his stupidity, *grieving* that he had made such a terrible mistake. He abjectly asked her *forgiveness* and *gave* her the rest of the week off. Maybe you can come up with a similar device to help you remember these necessary steps for restoring intimacy and allowing companionship to blossom once again.

CONFRONTATION

In chapter 5 you read of Tom and Laura who had trouble permitting truth and wisdom to shine into their lives and marriage. They were unable to confront the destructive patterns in their relationship. It wasn't until Tom was confronted by Laura, his pastor, and the stark reality of the situation, that he was able to recognize his own craziness.

It is great when partners all on their own are able to confront their own character defects or ineffective behaviors. Christ stated, "You will know the truth, and the truth will set you free" (John 8:32). But let's face it, most of us are not able to let God's light and truth shine into the dark, ineffective areas of our lives and marriages unless we are hit over the head with a two-by-four. We usually don't confront problems all on our own.

So often in counseling sessions I hear, "Why couldn't I have seen that and done something before things got so desperate? How could I have been so blind and stupid?" To which I reply, "That is the nature of blind spots. For some reason we cannot or do not want to see the truth." Oftentimes persons in counseling are still unaware of how much remains to be changed. They need additional confrontation as they further examine their own rough edges.

We all become better people for being in a good relationship because we are confronted and our character defects are sanded off. The Book of Proverbs reminds us of this, "As iron sharpens iron, so one man sharpens another. . . . Rebuke a wise man and he will love you. . . . Rebuke a discerning man and he will gain knowledge" (27:17; 9:8; 19:25). Nondefensive and effective confrontation is a vital part of intimate relationships. It promotes healing and growth. Though we don't enjoy it at the time, we are lucky to have people in our lives who love us enough to confront.

Remember Lisa who became frustrated with Jerry because her best shots at making him see his shortcomings miserably failed? Jerry got defensive and she got angry and he got angry and it disintegrated from there. Lisa had to learn that there is an art to confrontation — a person gently and strategically holds the mate's feet to the fire. The Apostle Paul gave wise advice on confrontation, "Correct, rebuke and encourage — with great patience and careful instruction" (2 Timothy 4:2).

When Jerry feels Lisa is in his corner and he is affirmed and encouraged, he will be less defensive and more open to exploring his defects and understanding where he is violating God's economy for intimacy. As Lisa can detach from and resolve her own resentment, she will be able to patiently confront. She will assertively communicate her needs and feelings in a careful, cooperative fashion. Together they can explore the scars and skill deficits that maintain his blind spots — gently confronting together.

If mates refuse to acknowledge or work on their rough edges, they need to consider the words of Christ about the act of confrontation: "If your brother sins against you, go and show him his fault, just between the two of you. If he listens to you, you have won your brother over. But if he will not listen, take one or two others along, so that every matter may be established by the testimony of two or three witnesses" (Matthew 18:15-16).

In the treatment of alcohol and drug dependence, a therapist and the family will often do an *intervention*. Anywhere from two to twelve important people who are in the addict's family and network will gather together and bluntly confront the individual about the destructive nature of his or her behavior. They will lay down consequences if the behavior continues.

Christ is advocating interventions. If a mate persists in sinful, ineffective behavior, the other one can bring in people who care, and together they can confront in a strategic fashion and establish a truthful, loving concensus. The mate who sees intimacy being destroyed can gently send the message, with the corroborating help of others: "I love you and don't want to be separated by this distancing behavior."

You may need to plan an intervention for your mate. Consult your pastor or counselor about your frustrations. This is a more positive plan of attack than the wife who told me, "I only see three things that have motivated my friends' husbands to change: an affair, a suicide attempt, or the threat of divorce." Surely we as Christians don't have to resort to these methods of confrontation.

● TIME OUT

1. When is confrontation ineffective for you? What causes you to get defensive the quickest? What could you do to make changes and be more open to confrontation?

2. Sit down with your mate and make up a list of rough edges you see in each other. Discuss your lists together and map out a strategy for attacking one of these trouble spots. Affirm and encourage one another!

REPENTANCE

Confrontation is part of God's economy to push toxic behaviors and attitudes into the recognition zone, but the other partner still has to acknowledge and accept responsibility. This is repentance: *admitting and understanding* how a behavior, like excessive busyness, has violated God's laws for companionship; and then, *making necessary changes* so the problem is healed and prevented from recurring.

It took Jenny a long time to see how harassed her marriage had become by their overinvolvement. Both she and Alex rationalized and avoided until it was almost too late. When they finally broke through the denial, they utilized their godly sorrow and fear to motivate them to make changes. They created goals in each area of their marriage: they decided to make Saturday afternoons sacred to their companionship and plan to do special things alone together. They covenanted to make love at least twice a week and carefully structured that into their busy schedule. They tried to understand better and resist the pressures of children, church, and careers.

Changing was difficult, but Alex and Jenny each personally accepted responsibility for getting their relationship back on track. They renewed their courtship behaviors and started doing the many little things again that had made them such great friends and lovers earlier in their marriage. They better understood God's admonition to the church at Ephesus: "I hold this against you: You have forsaken your first love. Remember the height from which you have fallen! Repent and do the things you did at first" (Revelation 2:4-5).

Their repentance efforts paid off as they daily acknowledged shortcomings and worked at keeping priorities in place. They proved "their repentance by their deeds" (Acts 26:20) as they rebuilt love and respect. Both started enjoying coming home again and looked forward to intimate times alone. Sometimes one or the other had to make the greater effort to keep intimacy progressing.

It is interesting how one partner can model repentance by accepting responsibility and starting to make changes. This can often shake up the whole marital system and encourage the other mate toward change. Alex experienced this when in the early stages of making changes he took the time to carve out a weekend together, only to have Jenny feel duty-bound to stay and work on the church music program. He was surprised that Friday to come home to a packed suitcase; Jenny had delegated her responsibility and was ready to go.

They were excited as time went by and their new behaviors became easier to follow through on. Healthier habits were solidly in place and they felt in love once again. Alex and Jenny strongly believed in the comments Paul made after he had confronted the Corinthians and they changed to align themselves back within God's economy, "Godly sorrow brings repentance that leads to salvation and leaves no regret" (2 Corinthians 7:10).

● **TIME OUT** _____

1. As we think of the companionship invaders, we know that repentance does not mean merely acknowledging the damage; it also means making healing changes. What have you acknowledged in your relationship, but not taken the courage and energy to change? How could you start?
2. Making changes is tough going. What are your favorite sabotages of the change process? How could you overcome them?

CONFESSION

Confession is a *strong healing agent* in the process of restoring damaged relationships. It has a key role in fostering repentant changes, encouraging forgiveness, and honestly making amends. It is modeled on God's promise, "If we confess our sins, He is faithful and just and will forgive us our sins" (1 John 1:9). All Christians are encouraged, "Confess your sins to each other and pray for each other so that you may be healed" (James 5:16). Confession has to be overt and intentional; "It is with your mouth that you confess" (Romans 10:10). The Greek word for *confession* carries the idea of "agreeing, saying alongside of." It is humbly agreeing with God's opinions that we have messed up His economy.

Think of what tremendous things will occur for Bruce and

his marriage when he tells Nancy, "I am sorry I have sat on so many of my resentful feelings and also have not exhibited my love enough. Please forgive me. In the future I will take the time and courage to express my anger, hurts, and love." Obviously, Bruce is agreeing with the scriptural injunctions of Ephesians 4 to "speak the truth in love" and "do not let the sun go down while you are angry," which he has violated.

In agreeing with God, Bruce is *clearing his spiritual channels and reestablishing his connection with the source of all healing*. He is humbly opening himself up to let God shine further truth into his life, as he clears garbage out and conforms more and more to His economy. He is allowing God to help him change character defects and find true intimacy.

Bruce is also bringing his hidden world of contaminating secrets and dishonesty into the light of day. This was what Norm did as he laid out all the ugliness of his adultery for Sandi. His unrevealed secrets seemed to gather destructive power as they contaminated, distanced, and invaded intimacy. *Confession brought these secrets out into the open and destroyed the sinful power*. Bruce and Norm both felt unshackled and experienced an amazing cleansing as they confessed to another human being their festering, secret world.

Norm also discovered that confession *relieves guilt and self-condemnation*. He found as he told his darkest secrets to another human being and saw that she still loved and accepted him, he experienced real healing. Somehow, in spite of what he had done, Sandi separated out his despicable actions from the person she loved. Confession gave to Norm this needed *affirmation that he was a good person who did bad things*.

Bruce and Norm needed confession to *feel forgiveness*. They knew that God promised to forgive any sin they confessed, but that other people helped them *experience* this forgiveness. As God's human representatives, their wives were able to say, "Neither do I condemn you, go and sin no more." The confession process emphasized the sorrow, repentance, and being accepted back into companionship. Norm felt hope, healing, cleansing, and restoring as Sandi listened and forgave.

A problem for Norm and his friend Bob, as well as for many making confessions, is how to accomplish the goals of reestablishing a relationship with God, getting the secrets out, and then experiencing acceptance in an *appropriate* fashion. Who is the right confessor and what is the proper setting?

• Confession should clean the channel to God and involve His appropriate agent, whether pastor, counselor, or perhaps mate.

• Confession should clear the air, destroy secrecy, and promote healing with the one or ones involved in the destructive secret. The sin should therefore be confessed to them, unless doing so would harm them. For example, sometimes a mate simply wants to share the guilt (a truly unloving act); a more appropriate confessor would be a minister or counselor.

• TIME OUT _____

1. Do you have appropriate confessors in your network: a best friend, minister, counselor, colleague? We need people who can hold us accountable in all areas of our lives, as they lovingly accept and encourage us. Can you think of a secret sin in your life that is building up steam? Who do you need to talk to?
2. Think of your marriage and the battering it often takes. What do you need to confess to your mate and seek healing for? What confession and repentant act would help clear the air and create renewed intimacy? Do it!

_____

EXPRESSION OF FEELINGS

People tell me that they know the Bible talks about God being angry, or hating, or being jealous, but that these feelings somehow seem wrong for them. In my conservative Christian background, I grew up thinking anger was wrong, or at least suspect. However, you will never heal a damaged marriage if you cannot express your strong feelings. Getting rid of anger, hatred, jealousy, and grief is vital to recovery.

Tom would have destructive temper tantrums, and he could be jealously possessive of Laura's time. These were obviously not godly expressions of the feelings of anger and jealousy. It would be easy to simplistically preach at Tom from Ephesians 4:31: "Get rid of all bitterness, rage and anger, brawling and slander, along with every form of malice," or from Proverbs 15:1: "A gentle answer turns away wrath, but a harsh word stirs up anger." But this is not the whole answer, because the Ephesians passage also says: "In your anger do not sin; do not let the sun go down while you are still angry" (v. 26). How then do we express these feelings? When are these strong feelings appropriate or inappropriate? Should we sit on them or let them out?

I believe we need to honestly express and deal with all feelings. Problems can enter in if we don't understand there are two kinds of feelings:

—*short-term, protective feelings* (anger, hatred, jealousy, grief) that God gives to us to help us work through difficult situations. As a result of sin in the world, we encounter injustice, death and losses, untrustworthiness and abuse.

—*long-term growth feelings* (love, joy, peace) that we cultivate as a part of intimacy and seek out over the long haul.

Take Tom's anger as an example. Anger is a God-given defense mechanism when we feel that justice has been violated; it is a signal that something is wrong in our life. It is not meant to be long-term or grow into bitterness, as it did in Bruce and Nancy's marriage. It is not meant to be expressed aggressively or develop into slander and rage. Anger is not to sleep on, but to be examined and dealt with. Why are we angry? On further examination, we may discover that justice has not been violated. Or, we may discover our toes have been stepped upon and we need to confront the issue, rather than avoiding or stuffing it.

Short-term feelings which are neglected can grow into long-term problems. A series of small injustices, for which the anger is stuffed and ignored, can erupt destructively a week or month later. The biblical principle of not letting the sun go down while you are angry is crucial to companionship. I know many couples who have saved their marriages many times over by making sure their differences are settled before they go to sleep.

Legitimate short-term jealousy or protectiveness of our mate can grow into possessiveness, and grief can grow into self-pity. Sandi had a right to suspect Norm's trustworthiness and explore her feelings toward him and Alison. In the short-term expression, jealousy is God's mechanism to protect what we value when our mates set poor boundaries or are not trustworthy. But if jealousy turns into possessiveness or constant suspicion, then it has become a destructive expression of a legitimate feeling.

We don't like people who abuse us; such dislike is normal and deserves expression. Deteriorating intimacy can create much pain and hatred. But this dislike should be a short-term feeling that we can eventually forgive and let go of. (The hatred of evil and wrong is a long-term emotion quite different from the short-term, protective feeling we are discussing here.)

No one likes to grieve and feel bad, but grief too is God's protective assistance for getting beyond and accepting the bad things that happen to us, and dealing with the losses that we all experience. The couples in chapters 1–5 had to polish up their grieving skills. They had to learn about the stages of grieving and realize that they would pop in and out of them as they slowly healed:

—*denial*—this isn't happening to me;

—*anger*—at myself, at God, at my mate, at life;

—*bargaining and interrogation*—does this have to happen? How can I change it? Why me?

—*depression*—sadness, crying over the loss, hopeless and helpless;

—*acceptance*—if I keep my boots on and keep wading, I will reach the other side; something bad has happened, but I will live wholly once again in the future.

● TIME OUT _____

1. Work on your feelings as you complete this sentence to your mate, for each of five feelings: "I feel angry (sad, loving, etc.) when. . . ."
2. What feeling can you express the best? When have you recently used a short-term feeling effectively? How did you express the feeling?

FORGIVENESS

Forgiveness can be a perplexing concept; usually the most difficult person to forgive is ourselves. The Bible makes forgiving an attitude or mind-set that every Christian should incorporate. "Do not judge . . . do not condemn . . . forgive, and you will be forgiven" (Luke 6:37). "Be kind and compassionate to one another, forgiving each other, just as in Christ God forgave you" (Ephesians 4:32). "Bear with each other and forgive whatever grievances you may have against one another" (Colossians 3:13).

Forgiveness seems to be a mature mind-set where you cut people some slack and do not hold grudges. It often is a personal process that is not dependent on the person who has hurt you.

It is your *letting go* of grievances so that they do not become a cancer of resentment and rage that eats you up. One woman who was kidnapped and raped was asked how she could forgive her rapist. She replied that he had gotten seven hours of her life and that was all he was getting. Forgiveness frees our emotional energy for better uses than resentment, grudges, or revenge.

Laura forgave Tom as he repented. She was confused though, because she seemed to have to repeat the process almost daily in the first few months. She slowly realized that *forgiveness is indeed a process.* Tom did not change immediately and he would reactivate the hurt so that a hidden pocket of resentment would float to the surface of her consciousness. She would forgive again and again and continue to work on herself and the marriage. She found it helped her to pray for Tom and for God's best in his life. This gave her better perspective: she could more easily leave him in God's hands and continue to forgive.

Norm was frustrated that Sandi did not forgive him and immediately let go of all her hate and resentment. He got tired of the forgiving and grieving process even though he knew great healing was taking place as she remembered, sorted through, and dealt with issues. He thought forgiving and instant forgetting were synonyms. This myth became quickly apparent. She could not trust him and constantly kept checking up on him and jumping him all over again.

As Norm slowly built a good track record, the forgetting increased. Claudia Black, an expert on survivors of sexual abuse, wisely tells her audiences, "Forgiving is not forgetting" but rather, "Forgiving is remembering and letting go." Louis Smedes in his book, *Forgive & Forget* states we have to hate and hurt before we can heal.[1] Sandi and Norm were having to go through this process.

Christ said, "If your brother sins, rebuke him, and if he repents, forgive him" (Luke 17:3). In the healing of a companionship, a mate can always let go of personal resentment, but the reestablishment of intimacy is stymied without repentance and a *mutual* forgiving process. A repentant attitude on the aggressor's part, and a loving, accepting mind-set on the forgiver's side, augments forgiveness and healing. "I'm sorry," and "I forgive you," go a long way.

Another necessary part of forgiving ourselves and our partners is understanding that forgiveness is never condoning what has happened. It is a personal "letting go" and placing the wrong in God's hands. Vengeance and ultimate consequence and correction are His domain. In forgiving, especially an unrepentant partner, we are trusting God to work with that person as we let go of our cancer of resentment. However, forgiveness is *not* opening yourself up to further abuse, but taking the self-protective steps God requires as you let go. Forgiving and turning the other cheek are not the same as condoning or advocating abusive or irresponsible behavior.

Sometimes a person remains unrepentant and refuses to see the hurt he or she is causing. We then have to grieve over the relationship we hoped to have but never may, as we make choices to protect ourselves and decide on the future. This protective action may not be divorce. It could include not sharing an activity with our mate we had hoped to share, or a separate checking account, or other action appropriate to the situation as we practice godly self-protection and a tough, confrontive love. It is important not to confuse forgiveness with forgetting, instant trust, or the enabling of ineffective behaviors.

---

1. Louis Smedes, *Forgive & Forget: Healing the Hurts We Don't Deserve*. San Francisco: Harper and Row Publisher, 1984, p. 2.

● TIME OUT _____

1. Is there someone in your life you have been unable to forgive? What is sabotaging forgiveness: have you hurt and hated, remembered so you can let go, grieved over broken hopes of a relationship you will never heal, trusted God to take vengeance? What are you gaining by not forgiving? What are you losing?
2. Would you describe forgiveness as an attitude or an action? What specific thing do you need to do right now to improve your forgiving attitude, to put forgiveness into action?

MAKING AMENDS

Alcoholics Anonymous considers making amends so important to successful recovery that they have made it one of their twelve essential steps for healing. Like the other concepts/ skills for healing damaged relationships, making amends has many facets and is a process over time. It can include everything from making apologies and asking forgiveness, taking time for therapy, resuming loving and romantic behaviors, to changing deeply ingrained character defects.

It is not unusual for the mate of a person involved in an extramarital affair to expect some sort of *restitution*. This seems a legitimate aspect of making amends. When the chief tax collector Zaccheus came to Christ, he stated he was going to make fourfold amends for what he had taken from the people. Making amends means providing restitution in a way that is restorative and healing; it does not cause further resentment, anger, and hurt. Sandi wanted Norm to commit to therapy and spend extra amounts of time with her as they tried to reclaim intimacy, and to patiently deal with her doubts and interrogation. This seemed fair to Norm.

Making amends *restores trust and encourages loving connectedness*. It *exacts some sense of restitution and decreases anger and the need for vengeance,* as justice is restored. It *demonstrates humility and loving repentance* as energy is expended to nurture the victimized mate and marriage. It is a tangible way of demonstrating, "I'm sorry and I want this to work." Making amends also *deals with guilt* and *helps the offending partner experience a greater feeling of forgiveness and healing,* as he or she completes their penance.

Part of Bruce and Nancy's amends to each other and their relationship was a very painful process of opening old wounds and patiently trying to affirm commitment, when they really felt like running. Later Bruce made a special effort to do the little romantic gestures Nancy used to love, like breakfast in bed, even though she was unpredictable in her reception of these gestures. He quickly saw that restitution and amends would not always be a warm, happy process.

Norm's friend Bob also experienced making amends as he apologized to those he had hurt in his adulterous behavior. He did this carefully, with Jill's assistance, so he did not excite any more hurt or jealousy in her and did not injure any innocent party further. Like other healing skills, making amends must be done appropriately. The goal of the process is overcoming guilt, making restitution, restoring respect and trust, and rebuilding.

● TIME OUT

1. When was the last time you made amends? Who do you need to go to in addition to your mate? What steps could you take today to start making amends to your partner? Discuss it with him or her.
2. Sit down with your mate and practice the art of apologizing for at least fifteen minutes. Let one of you start and then switch back and forth as each apologizes for offenses and clears the air. Concentrate on the attitude of love, empathy, and humility rather than just the words.

FOR FURTHER READING

Harriet Goldhor Lerner, *Dance of Anger*. New York: Harper and Row Publishers, 1985.

James Dobson, *Love Must Be Tough*. Dallas: Word Publishing Company, 1983.

Gordon MacDonald, *Rebuilding Your Broken World*. Nashville: Oliver-Nelson, 1988.

CHAPTER SEVEN

Defining a Great Marriage

✠

*M*arriage disappoints many people. I remember one woman who looked forward to being married and experiencing a great sexual relationship. Unfortunately, her romantic expectations fell flat. She told me, "It was like I went out to purchase a brand-new Cadillac and came home with a camel." She certainly is not alone.

What are those couples doing right who are enjoying their marital companionship? Disappointment is certainly not where anyone wants to stay. Most effective partnerships have begun to master three critical tasks. It may help you remember these three processes by the mnemonic device: Extremely Great Party. Happy couples have slowly worked through to realistic marital *Expectations.* They have created specific, achievable *Goals* from these expectations. These goals are then *Prioritized* and accomplished. It is wonderful when marriage becomes an Extremely Great Party.

EXPECTATIONS

Nancy was surprised and troubled as she realized Bruce had quite different ideas than she did about the husband's role in handling the financial responsibilities of marriage. She assumed most happy couples would be similar to her parents. Her mom had an excellent head for business matters and always had investments and property of her own. Her dad was proud of her mom's financial skills and independence and counted on her to keep the checkbook balanced. He respected the great partnership they made.

Bruce thought he should make all important decisions and, as the breadwinner, should have the major role in any financial transaction; he did not feel a need to consult Nancy. She was glad he wasn't a spendthrift; if anything, he was probably too tight. But she had good business skills which Bruce was not including in the relationship. The need for joint financial decisions had not occurred in their dating days, but now with their buying a new car, Nancy was ready to put her foot down.

Bruce felt equally confused because he thought women appreciated nurturing leadership. This was so different from his mom who did not want a part in any financial hassles or the purchase of a car. She trusted his dad's judgment. This was not the only area where he had been disappointed in marriage, but it was certainly the worst so far. He was a neatnik and Nancy had a much higher tolerance of mess; also, he thought all women were great cooks, and she wasn't. Confusion over expectations and ideals abounded, with the car becoming very symbolic.

Nancy and Bruce fought and cried and felt miserable for over a week before they were able to begin to understand the other's background, reality, and expectations. It was tough on them because they both felt they were making such logical points; it was rather like Bruce's computer was using BASIC language when Nancy was programmed for COBOL. The conflict never was completely resolved, but Bruce recognized her need/expectation to be respected for her financial skills and to be consulted on all major decisions. Nancy better understood Bruce's desire to protect and lead and to take the role of husband very seriously.

Most couples enter marriage with a variety of expectations about how it should be. Where do we get these ideals and prototypes of the perfect marriage? Our family of origin is a big factor, including the way our parents modeled marriage. Society and our peer groups communicate many messages about romance and the good life. We have gone from Doris Day movies and "Leave It to Beaver" into "Roseanne," "Bill Cosby," and "The Simpsons." Our religious teachings also have tremendous impact. Bruce was trying to make sense of the concept of the husband being head of the home, while Nancy pondered her own God-given skills and autonomy. Our gender, personality differences, and uniqueness contribute to our expectations, as well as the uniqueness of each of our parents. Bruce's mom was more passive, while Nancy's modeled high energy and a quick mind for figures.

I encounter many couples whose unrealistic expectations have hampered their happiness and their marital intimacy. How many of the following expectations have you experienced?

- We would eat dinner together at the table most nights.
- He would automatically take the garbage out and vacuum.
- We never would fight.
- She/he wouldn't jump up immediately after sex and run to the bathroom.
- He would be excited about the pregnancy.
- He would be a great lover/know about investments/ open up and share his feelings.
- We would share everything and be the best of friends.
- He or she would never be attracted to anyone else.
- Sex would be instantly available and I would never be lonely.
- We would have joint checking accounts.
- We wouldn't go to his mom's every Sunday for dinner.
- Thanksgiving would be spent with my family.

Sometimes, couples tell me that if they could let go of expectations, they would have happy, fulfilling marriages. I ask them, "Why get married if you don't expect anything from it?" No, I think the task we all face is to sort out the unrealistic from the realistic expectations. For example, I believe it is unrealistic to think that there will never be conflict in a marriage. What is realistic is to expect that conflict will lead to resolution, and contribute to growth in a relationship.

EIGHT UNREALISTIC EXPECTATIONS
Important aspects of resolving unrealistic expectations are the communication and confrontation skills needed for a couple to successfully work beyond them. These skills will be dis-

cussed in chapter 10. For now, here are eight unrealistic expectations; many couples bring three or four of these into their marriage. Looking at these can help you discover and confront your own.

1. *Strong relationships have few disagreements.* Two unique, autonomous people will certainly disagree and have conflict. I worry when couples say they never fight. I fear they aren't assertively expressing their needs and feelings, or risking necessary confrontation. They may be sitting on a lot of disappointed expectations which will erupt at some point.

2. *One person can meet all my needs and make me happy.* I remember the time a single person told me I was lucky to be married because I had sex instantly available and I was never lonely. My wife and I now kid each other about this comment. God intended for us to have our sexual needs met within marriage, but sex is never instantly available. Also, He certainly never intended one person to meet all our needs from tennis buddy to mentor and sounding board to only best friend and antidote to loneliness. It is unrealistic to expect someone else to make us happy. We have a personal responsibility for that; no person can be expected to meet all our emotional needs all of the time.

3. *Sex equals intercourse equals intimacy.* Couples can focus on always pursuing intercourse and orgasm, rather than holding, hugging, and playing together. Sexual pleasure is diminished if it is just the pursuit of an orgasm. Many couples put an unrealistic burden on their sex life for creating and maintaining intimacy. With some men, sex is their only avenue for letting down and sharing intimate feelings. Sex should flow out of intimate companionship and enjoy much greater variety than just intercourse.

4. *Effective relationships have little need for structure and boundaries.* Every great marriage is based on commitment and needs appropriate structure to protect the companionship. Busy couples will never have the quality of life they desire unless they plan, organize, and keep their priorities. Discipline and boundaries are *vital* for any relationship to thrive. To paraphrase Robert Frost, good fences make good marriages.

5. *My mate will be similar to me in values, thinking, and*

needs. It is such a shocking experience when it sinks in that our mate doesn't think and feel just like we do. A second great shock is when we discover they are also not similar to our parents. They may not think football is fun, sex is great after a fight, money should be saved, or Christmas vacation should be spent with family.

6. *Great marriages have total sharing.* In marriage or any close relationship, there needs to be some mystery and the right to some private spaces. A mate who shares everything, and has what some people call "total honesty," may destroy the marriage. Our mates just aren't that excited about our previous relationships or how badly their clothes fit. I will not burden my wife with every lustful or confusing thought. I do not demand she assume roles that should be met by my buddy of the same sex. Mates often need affirmation more than total sharing: "Your hair looks great." "Pregnant is beautiful."

7. *A partnership means sharing everything equally.* Some mates are so defensive about keeping everything equally shared that they sacrifice building a partnership. He may love to cook, she may be adept at balancing a checkbook, or she may need the mountains more than he needs the beach. A loving partnership may see a compromise as 100/0 rather than 50/50. Many people are comfortable only when the debit/credit balance is at 50/50 or they are giving more than they receive. A mutually nurturing companionship needs more than this.

8. *Marriage is the ultimate experience.* Marriage does not create a total identity for a person. We are more than husband or wife. Marriage is not the total antidote to boredom nor does it provide an instant, complete support network. It does not guarantee great sex or children who are an automatic blessing. Marriage does not ensure economic stability or fewer problems in life. Marriage is a supportive relationship, *not* magic or a cure-all.

EIGHT REALISTIC EXPECTATIONS

You may be discouraged after reading the unrealistic ideals and wonder what marriage has to offer. God's special covenant relationship has limitless potential. Here are eight realistic expectations that all mates deserve from this powerful partnership. Don't settle for less.

1. I have a lifetime companion and soulmate. Marriage is intended for the long haul and provides a special meaning and purpose in life. It is fun to have a mate to make plans with for the future as you cherish each present moment. Couples build up a special shared history, creating traditions and warm memories together. They become playmates. It is realistic to expect a partner to share your soul and to warmly connect. Lisa had a right to know what Jerry was thinking and feeling and to be included in his life.

2. I can expect regular and satisfying sexual interaction. Both mates deserve to have their sexual needs met. A husband or wife can expect to have a spouse who lovingly helps him or her achieve a personal sexual satisfaction in a mutually nurturing way. It is also realistic to expect an intimacy-enhancing sexual connectedness that grows over the years — a sexual communication that is much more than just intercourse or orgasm. This will require an investment to ensure time, provide variety, and avoid ruts.

3. The marriage relationship is not labor-intensive. Something is wrong if couples are unable to resolve the conflicts in their marriages. Hear me carefully: all couples have craziness and incompatibility in various areas; there will be conflict and a need for patience and hard work. But working hard is different than laboring intensely. God wants marital intimacy to grow into joyfulness, peacefulness, and to become a comfortable place to regroup. It is not unrealistic to want a relationship where we can relax. It is our imperative mission to mutually find out what is wrong and make changes if it is not this way. All mates need some smooth, trouble-free sailing and times of resting comfortably at anchor in a peaceful harbor.

4. I will have a faithful, committed partner. Commitment takes daily work to properly maintain it. Such work may be, as Norm had to learn, a choice to guard one's sexual thought life or refuse a potentially dangerous situation. Dependable partners don't cheat. It may be learning to say no to new obligations and to jealously guard time together. It may be setting goals and maintaining priorities. A growing, intimate marriage demands *commitment,* sexual loyalty, and the gifts of time and energy.

5. *I will have a constantly changing mate and marriage.* The reasons that we married our partner are not always strong enough to keep us together for a lifetime. We can continually develop deeper love and attachments. Who we are today may be very different from who we are five years from now. Mates discover new things about themselves constantly. A vibrant relationship is an open system that welcomes new ideas and tries different behaviors. A marriage that is not committed to the growth and change process gets in a deepening rut of boredom and frustration.

6. *My marriage is a total package.* I do not like the idea that marriage is a hierarchy with Jesus first, our mate second, our family third, work fourth, and our mother-in-law tenth. I think a more realistic model of marriage is a big apple pie. Our relationship with God and His economy is the all-encompassing and stabilizing pie plate. Our children are a piece of the pie, our time alone together is a piece of the pie, our careers are a piece, our leisure activities are a piece, etc.

One angry stepmother in my office vehemently stated, "It is either me or his children." A confused husband demanded, "She gives up her career or the marriage is over." To both I quickly stepped in and said, "Whoa! This is an impossible demand. You will destroy your mate and marriage if you try to make them throw out an essential piece of the pie." We can lessen the size of the piece of the pie or choose to set boundaries and deal with it differently. Throughout our marriage various slices of the pie will grow in importance or time demands. As I write this book, my career slice is three-fourths of the pie time-wise, but certainly not in importance.

7. *I have a partner in my corner.* In a boxing match, the boxer has in his corner a manager who is unconditionally committed to help him utilize his best shots, encourage, confront, take care of wounds, and prepare him for maximum efficiency. We can expect to become better persons in a solid marital relationship. We have an ally to help us realize our potential as we discover our strengths and correct our weaknesses.

8. *I deserve quality playtime!* An intimate relationship

should enjoy play, humor, laughter, excitement, and fun. We started off with the realistic expectation that mates should be lifetime companions and soulmates. Let me conclude with the idea that the companionship should include a lot of fun and quality playtime. That can range from an exciting sex life to mutual hobbies, from concerts to backpacking, from travel to watching videos together. Sometimes one or both will have to fight that misguided notion that they don't deserve fun, and let each mate learn to relax and play.

● TIME OUT _____

1. Together with your mate, name two expectations you got from your parents and other family relationships. Which of the listed unrealistic expectations do you struggle with the most?
2. Make a list of the top four expectations you have for your marriage. They may have been triggered by the ideas in this chapter or be different. Share them with your mate. Discuss their importance to you; suggest possible modifications.

_____

GOALS

Unrealistic expectations kill potentially great marriages. Many marriages flounder because a couple's realistic expectations are never translated into specific, realizable goals. Norm and Sandi were zooming along with a satisfying companionship, but they had never specified how they would preserve and enrich that marital friendship. They had not structured an adequate support network to advise and encourage them, or found ways to effectively use their leisure time. This lack of goals set them up for adultery.

● CHARACTERISTICS OF AN EFFECTIVE GOAL. A goal that is going to get the job done should be *specific, realistic and attainable, and scheduled.* Clients will often tell me they intend to love their mate better or be nicer or try to talk more. I encourage them to be more *specific* and set up actual behavioral steps as they focus on a given area— behaviors like talking fifteen minutes after the kids are in bed, taking the garbage out without being asked, planning a dinner party for her birthday, or initiating sex on Tuesday evenings.

The goals should start with small steps that are *realistic and attainable*. A husband will say, "We are going to have family devotions every night for a half hour." A more realistic start might be fifteen minutes on Monday and Thursday evenings when they all eat dinner together, or perhaps sharing a short reading and prayer with his wife every night at 9 o'clock, regardless of what both are doing. Goals that are not reasonable and do not consider time, energy, and money demands will quickly be sabotaged.

Finally, goals need to have a *schedule* so they can be implemented. "We are going to take walks more often" will probably fall by the wayside. But a goal of walking right after supper the two week nights they are home and on Sunday afternoon, starting this week, will more likely get done. "We will make love with greater frequency" is attainable and fairly specific, but "We will make love every Tuesday night and Sunday morning" is behaviorally very specific and can be scheduled.

● GOAL-SETTING. Some goals will be more *personal* even though they have a definite impact on the relationship like, "I will count to ten before angrily spouting off," or "I will work out every Monday and Thursday evening." Other goals will be more directly *relational* like, "We will start building a better baby-sitting network, by asking the teenage girl across the street her availability this Thursday night and every Thursday night." In a good marriage the personal and relational often blend together: "We will plan one-week vacations every August and around New Year's Day."

Now comes the tough part, working through the goal-setting chart on page 96! Take a blank sheet of paper and divide it in half, then to eighths and write the topic headings from the chart in each block. Such exercises are tough to discipline yourself to do. Yet they are most helpful in enriching or healing a marriage. Block out a couple of evenings or take a weekend to create your goals.

I chose these *eight topics* because they are the areas where I encounter the most misunderstandings and conflict in coun-

Eight Marriage Priorities for Setting
Specific, Realistic, and Scheduled Goals

MONEY: Budget, Priorities, Insurance 1. 2.	SEX: Frequency, Enrichment, Boundaries 1. 2.
FAMILY: Children, Parents 1. 2.	SPIRITUALITY: Personal, Church, Relational 1. 2.
WORK: Career, Home duties, Volunteer 1. 2.	COMPANIONSHIP: Communication, Time alone, Activities 1. 2.
SUPPORT NETWORK: Friends, Sitters, Groups 1. 2.	LEISURE TIME: Exercise, Vacations, Hobbies 1. 2.

1. Create one personal goal and one relational goal in each of these areas.

2. Place a plus (+) by the three goals on this chart that need priority—to be tackled first.

3. Place a minus (-) by the three goals that seem least important.

4. Place an (x) by the goals you think your partner listed similar to yours.

seling married couples. They are also vital to a great marriage. Money causes so many fights because of differing values and needs. Sex can enhance a marriage or make it miserable. Children and family bring great joy but also dampen intimacy. Spiritual growth is crucial to all of the other areas as we develop a personal relationship with God. Work can encompass everything from developing a career track, to home chores, to taking time away from the marriage to help at a shelter for the homeless. Companionship is at the core of intimacy. Unfortunately, great communication and romantic time alone don't simply happen. Your support network extends from a best friend to a Bible study group to your personal marriage counselor for that six month checkup. Leisure time is one of the most important elements of the well-being of any individual or relationship; to neglect this is to doom your marriage to drudgery, boredom, and poor health.

Now that you and your mate have created goals in these eight crucial areas, let me make an invaluable suggestion. Go away for a weekend and plan out blocks of time for a total of at least six uninterrupted hours to work on your marital goals. Patricia and Julian Harwell are good friends of mine who have been an inspiration to me in the area of marriage and goal-setting. Patricia is a marriage and family therapist and she and Julian truly practice what they preach. Every year in the fall before the holiday rush, they reserve a weekend and go to a peaceful, romantic setting. It is a time they eagerly anticipate.

They pray and relax and have time for quiet meditation as well as discussion. Because they do this every year, they begin by reviewing last year's goals individually and together. They think through how well they have been achieved and whether some should be modified and carried over. They try to keep their goals very specific and attainable within a year's time.

Patricia and Julian then separately create new goals for the coming year and come back for joint discussion and feedback. They lovingly ponder and pray over each goal as they try to amend or improve them as needed. It turns into a very bonding and rewarding weekend that annually provides a marvelous encouragement to their companionship. The goals provide a framework to build a more meaningful lifestyle and marriage that is disciplined, joyful, and productive. I appreciate the wise stewardship Julian and Patricia model. Such goal-setting can revolutionize your marriage.

PRIORITIZING GOALS

Danger! Warning! It is not enough just to set goals for your marriage. These objectives will have to be *protected* from sabotage and *accomplished* before an enjoyable, intimate lifestyle can be achieved. In a practical, commonsense fashion, your goals have to be prioritized at the same time you create a lifestyle that encourages their accomplishment.

• A SELECTIVE COVENANT PROCESS. Most people are not that different from Alex and Jenny, the couple who stayed guilt-ridden and harassed, vowing they needed a better quality of life and fearing their intimate companionship was slipping away. They spent so much time taking care of emergencies, putting out fires, or procrastinating that many things important to them and their marriage never got done. They lived in a general state of frustration.

Alex and Jenny tried to set goals, but old habits were hard to change and their best attempts fizzled. In their growing desperation, they finally employed a major principle in setting and achieving objectives: create priorities. They chose a limited number of goals. They then selected three to accomplish in the coming year, come what might. These three were: Refusing any more responsibilities at church or school; going away for a three-day weekend every two months; saving $3,000.

This time Alex and Jenny were finally on the right track. They had prioritized their goals and jointly covenanted together that they would accomplish them. Like Alex and Jenny, my wife, Cathy, and I carefully thought through and chose the writing of this book as a priority goal. Other things might get put on hold, but the book would be completed. For many years I have wanted to author a book but somehow, like buying a house, having a child, or starting a savings account, the right time never seemed to come along.

The other day as I sat slaving over another chapter, Cathy told me how tired she was of my book. I listened empathetically to her feelings and commiserated with her. I too hated writing six hours every day of our summer vacation. Taking my day off on Friday as well as much of Sunday to write was truly getting old. I told her maybe I should quit for the afternoon and go grocery shopping, one of my usual Friday chores. She immediately put her foot down and told me I was going to stay at that desk for at least two more hours. We were going to get this book done; she would continue to take up the slack and help in any way possible. You can see we made our goal.

Oldtime evangelist Bob Jones used to exhort, "Never sacrifice the permanent on the altar of the immediate." But it takes real work to prioritize goals and follow through on them. Resisting emergencies and refusing to procrastinate is difficult; you must refuse to get sucked into the urgent rat race. Remember, limit your goals and raise them to the category of A-1 priority as you covenant together to accomplish them.

● CREATING A LIFESTYLE AND MIND-SET. Alex and Jenny still struggled even after prioritizing their short-term goals. They had so much going on and Jenny was a perfectionist. Alex was in the midst of long hours in an important career move, and the children demanded attention. Slowly their goals began to be sabotaged, and they sought further help in maintaining their priorities. Together we established a plan of action for helping them better follow through on their covenanted goals.

1. Simplify lifestyle. They had to learn to say no to new commitments and make their "no" stick. They avoided complicating relationships and were better able to set limits with their parents around weekly visits. Jenny streamlined the household chores with Alex and the children helping out. Alex set up guidelines for work demands and jealously guarded time at home. Some things had to go and others were put off, corners were cut, and *simplify* became their operative word.

2. Accept second best; be comfortable with loose ends. Jenny and Alex struggled with wanting to do everything perfectly. She had to learn that if there were six household chores needing attention, two or three of them would have to be done halfway or quickly. One of my mentors, Dr. Haddon Robinson, used to say, "If a job is worth doing, it is worth doing poorly," especially if your choice is doing it that way or not at all. Accepting a B grade in that night course, dusting only the visible places, eating ordered pizza, or staying only a half hour at Mom's became Alex and Jenny's efforts at accepting second best but keeping their priorities. They got more comfortable as they gave themselves permission to leave some tasks undone or half-done. Alex and Jenny slowly progressed beyond their discomfort with loose ends and lived more comfortably with ambiguity. They tried to leave situations in God's hands as they pursued their goals and practiced the Serenity Prayer: "God grant me the serenity to accept the things I cannot change, courage to change the things I can, and wisdom to know the difference."

3. *Build a support network.* Alex and Jenny learned they needed to delegate some emergencies, busywork, or needed chores. The children became better organized; sister Joan took care of Mom's broken hip; a maid once a week did vacuuming and the bathrooms. They even used each other more wisely as support. A solid network became an important part of achieving their priorities.

4. *Keep focused on priorities and set up red flags.* Alex put a list of his yearly priority goals on the back of the medicine cabinet mirror and reviewed them daily. Both he and Jenny realized they had not done a good job of keeping their goals on the front burner of their minds and lives. This realization, in itself, was important.

Together in therapy and at home they thought through what would be the easiest way to sabotage each of their goals and erected red warning flags that would alert them to potential dangers. For example, Alex was going to jog three times a week when he came home from work. His red flag was if he missed two jogging sessions in a two-week span, something was wrong and he was starting to sabotage and would explore why. One of their mutual goals was to save $3,000 this year. They chose to check every four months that they had saved $1,000 and, if not, carefully budget for a month to make up any deficit.

Jenny and Alex got excited as they changed their lifestyle,

set up red flags, and started reaching their goals. As in any process, the successes snowballed and they found it easier to keep focused on their goals. Sabotages were reduced, and the quality of their intimacy dramatically increased.

CHAPTER EIGHT

Christian Selfness and the Healing of Codependency

✠

*K*yle came into my office all fired up to begin the counseling process and make revolutionary changes in his marriage. He had felt unhappy for a long time. A dynamic sermon the previous Sunday on the fun and friendship of a great marriage encouraged him to begin building better intimacy. He wondered if he had ever felt in love with Candy—the past years were a blur of work, debts, disappointments, and increasing alienation. He and Candy led very scattered, undisciplined lives and were given to depressive mood swings that brought them both down. He disliked many aspects of his job but stuck with it, not sure of what changes to make.

I am afraid I deflated Kyle's balloon of instant miracles in his marriage when I stated, "Your marriage is never going to work until you get your act together." We then began exploring the concept that a solid relationship is built on two whole people who know who they are and like themselves. Kyle needed to take control of his life and to gain self-esteem as he overcame some of the codependent craziness he had brought into the relationship.

This seemed a very selfish process to Kyle, as it does to many Christians. He thought he should focus outside himself on Candy and their interaction, not on himself. I reassured him that though it seemed confusing, there were two bottom-line components to dynamic, intimate companionship: *selfishness and unselfishness.* The journey to becoming one flesh often begins with working on ourselves.

The Bible stresses the importance of self-love. Those who do not love themselves are incapable of loving others. The standard by which we are to love and nurture our mate is based on how we are to love and nurture ourselves. "Love your neighbor as yourself" (Mark 12:31); "husbands ought to love their wives as their own bodies" (Ephesians 5:28). These commandments have little meaning to us if we lack self-esteem and a healthy focus on ourselves as individuals.

Christian mates are also autonomous individuals who are responsible for themselves and their own spiritual and emotional growth. They should feel good about their strength to challenge situations and change their own defects. Individuals have power and identity apart from their marriage identity. "Each one should test his own actions. Then he can take pride in himself, without comparing himself to somebody else, for each one should carry his own load" (Galatians 6:4). "Continue to work out your salvation" (Philippians 2:12). "For God did not give us a spirit of timidity, but a spirit of power, of love and of self-discipline" (2 Timothy 1:7).

Kyle went home from his first session redirected to do some self-esteem and identity homework. He also understood how he and Candy would have to address the other component of marriage: unselfishness. Deep intimacy would be built on considerately nurturing Candy and reaching out beyond himself, as he subordinated his needs for her good. He needed to humbly walk in her moccasins as they mutually trusted and supported each other. "Love is patient, love is kind. . . . It is not rude, it is not self-seeking. . . . It always protects, always trusts, always hopes, always perseveres" (1 Corinthians 13:4-7). "Submit to one another out of reverence for Christ" (Ephesians 5:21). "Do nothing out of selfish ambition or vain conceit, but in humility consider others" (Philippians 2:3). "Carry each other's burdens, and in this way you will fulfill the law of Christ" (Galatians 6:2).

As we have considered the couples attacked by the marriage dragons, we have seen that their marriages were also hurt by an inability to successfully incorporate both a healthy unselfishness and selfishness. Tom neglected to reach out and meet Laura's needs, but he also failed to selfishly work on his own craziness. Jenny got so involved with the children and homemaking she lost herself and became a dull, fatigued companion. Norm involved himself in affairs and refused to submit his needs for the good of the marriage. He quit seeking a trusting, mutually enriching companionship with his wife, Sandi. After Norm's affair, Sandi thought something must be wrong with her and wondered if she was desirable and lovable. Her self-concept plummeted and she withdrew from intimacy.

These examples show that balance must somehow be created between companionship and autonomy, between dependence and independence, between self-love and submission, between a reaching out and a looking inward. This chapter explores the self part of the equation, while chapter 14 carefully encourages the journey of becoming one-flesh companions.

I often use words like *self-esteem, responsibility, self-awareness, self-love,* and *self-direction* rather than *selfishness.* I realize Christians are often so afraid of negative, sinful selfishness that they avoid the whole concept. For that reason, I have coined the word *selfness* to talk about this important topic of self-esteem and self-directedness.

FOUR PITFALLS OF SELFNESS

I don't want to sound naive or simplistic—I see many marriages that are severely damaged by destructive selfishness and the teachings of the Me Generation as well as by ineffective Christianity. I commonly encounter four sabotages that allow selfness to hinder rather than enhance intimacy.

● AN END IN ITSELF, AS ULTIMATE MEANING. Self-esteem and a secure self-concept are means to an end, not an end in themselves. The better I feel about Doug, the easier it is for me to forget about myself and truly reach out and enjoy life and relationships. I do not create a good body image, or accept how God has made me, just to boost my ego. I want to accept myself so I can be unself-conscious as I interact with others. Self-esteem is curious: we try to get it only so we can then forget about it.

I cringe when a mate says, "I've got to be me. I need to leave this marriage so I can find myself." The Me Generation has become very impoverished and self-defeating by their quest for personal meaning to the exclusion of all else. All of us are guilty of this now and again, as we make ourselves the center of the universe to our own detriment. The Creator of the universe designed His economy so we will never find ultimate meaning unless we are willing to reach out beyond ourselves and build loving relationships with God and other people. Self-awareness and self-esteem are simply tools and a means to an end, not the ultimate meaning and purpose in life.

• SELF-ISOLATION. There are many lonely, miserable people in life to whom selfness means being a solitary island. It may be like Brenda, trapped in her timidness with trouble reaching out; or insecure Josie who doesn't think anyone, including his wife, would want to be his friend; or Tom whose own craziness isolated him. God created us with the need and ability for intimate relationships. Yes, we will always feel a little lonely, because no human being can ever be there for us all of the time. But selfness gives us opportunity to intimately connect; it does not doom us to isolation. Intimacy is the antidote to loneliness, and this chapter will help individuals avoid the isolation pitfall as they get their own act together and build more intimate companionships.

I feel sad when people remain islands because they have to protect their freedom and autonomy so closely. They rule out and fear commitment and intimacy as being too smothering. Laura felt this about Tom as she struggled through her midlife crisis. Fortunately, as she chafed at responsibility and restrictions, she slowly realized that ultimate freedom would leave her without her daughter, her job, or Tom, and yield a very meaningless existence. In God's economy, island living gets boring and lonely very quickly.

• SELF-CENTEREDNESS. There is a type of selfishness that is just plain old preoccupation with our own needs and an unwillingness to empathize with or nurture someone else. This is a part of sinful human nature and has existed long before the Me Generation. Greed, envy, insecurity, false-pride, and laziness all exalt the importance of our own needs and play havoc with intimacy. They are not a part of healthy selfness. Self-centeredness can be quite subtle and come under the guise of caretaking, a bleeding heart, the martyr, or being fragile or supersensitive. True self-esteem does away with all forms of self-centeredness.

● SELF-DEMOTION. Some Christian interpretations of submission and humility have created wimps, doormats, and timid, servile spouses. Jenny in chapter 1 was so busy being supermom, submitting her needs to endless Christian service, and trying to take care of Alex that she lost all perspective. I dislike the acrostic JOY standing for Jesus first, others second, and yourself last. Others and yourself have to be balanced or your neighbor will be treated as shabbily as you treat yourself.

Christians are sometimes so intent on subjecting and repressing all of their own needs that they rob others of the privilege of nurturing them and getting to know them as unique individuals. You are not doing yourself or your mate a favor if you always reply, "Whatever is the least trouble," or "I don't care, make yourself happy," or "Whatever you want to do." Healthy selfness lets us express our unique needs and be interesting individuals without resorting to wimpiness, dull anonymity, or an immobilizing fear of being selfish.

SEVEN FUNDAMENTALS OF SELF-ESTEEM

A lack of self-esteem is at the root of so many individual and relational problems. In looking at some of the pitfalls in working on a healthy selfness concept, we have already begun addressing what self-esteem is all about and how its absence can be devastating. Sandi's lack of self-esteem caused her to blame herself and feel very undesirable because of Norm's affair, rather than to see the situation for what it was. Tom grew crazier in his interactions with Laura and had no perspective on what was possible in an intimate relationship, because of his deep insecurity dating back to childhood traumas. Lisa got angry and had no way of securing accurate feedback on whether she or Jerry was dropping the ball. She just knew she kept withdrawing more and reaching out less.

What do Sandi, Tom, and Lisa need to do to build self-esteem so they can securely reach out beyond themselves to intimately reconnect with their mates? Here are seven foundational blocks upon which the ability to feel good about ourselves is built; seven fundamentals of self-esteem which Sandi, Tom, Lisa, you, and I can practice so we can reach out beyond ourselves in love and service.

1. Relationship to God. Every person is created by God in His image and is a special and worthwhile person. As the saying goes, "God don't make no junk." The Psalmist David said that God knew him even before he was born and carefully made him a unique creation in his mother's womb. "I praise You because I am fearfully and wonderfully made" (Psalm 139:14). We are all fearfully and wonderfully made. The bottom line of self-esteem is agreeing with God's opinion of us. So often we slap Him in the face and believe ourselves worthless or unlovable. God and we are a majority and we should be able to securely rest in this majority opinion.

God also offers us the opportunity to be in a special redemptive relationship with Himself in which He helps us slowly become more Christlike and do fewer dumb and/or sinful things. To be rightly related to Him gives us a special meaning and purpose in life. He will help our self-concept as He brings out the best in us, if we are willing to conform to His will and His way.

● TIME OUT _____

1. Write on a sheet of paper ten times, "I, _____, am a special and important person." Say this to someone else and to yourself out loud, looking in a mirror. How do you slap God in the face? Do you accept your body image, your personality, your needs?
2. How would your self-esteem improve if you trusted God more and conformed to His economy?

---

2. Self-acceptance. This foundational stone piggybacks on the first one; it is the ability not only to accept God's verdict but also to truly know ourselves. We need to discover, accept, and build on our *strengths* while we minimize our *limitations.* Let me give you a personal example. It was the first time I had seen this couple and I was exuberant to have gotten them as clients, because their marital needs were right down my alley. I burst out, "I'm glad you found me. I'll be great for what you need. I excel at teaching communication skills." On paper that seems mild and reassuring and not that egotistic, but unbeknown to me, this couple was a little taken aback. They talked about it on the way home from the session and wondered if I wasn't too proud of my skills and tooting my own horn. It troubled their Christian conviction that "pride comes before a fall."

Fortunately, they came back and confronted me with their misgivings. We switched the topic from communication skills to self-esteem and talked about the difference between pride/arrogance and self-confidence. We worked through the fact that pride, unlike self-confidence, is often not rooted in reality and is based on insecurity or a need to manipulate. I apologized for any misunderstanding and assured them that if I had told them I was going to sing a first-rate solo at my church the next Sunday, that would have been arrogance. But I felt I had a gift for teaching, and the feedback I received was that I taught communication concepts well. We went from there into a listing of their gifts and abilities. I had them brag on themselves and affirm all that God had given them as they truly accepted themselves.

● TIME OUT

1. Take a job you have done well in the past month and dissect the abilities that have helped you accomplish it.
2. What personal limitations did you have to minimize? How did your limitations help you? Do you accept and thank God for them? The Apostle Paul was able to be appreciative of his (2 Corinthians 11–12).

---

3. *Taking action.* Eric lacked self-confidence. His insecurity kept him stuck in a very frustrating job and provoked his wife, Lucia, to be confrontive about his timid, passive approach to life. He just seemed so predictable and dull. But he started making changes when he began to accept his

strengths and abilities and understand his limitations. Then came a tough part of building self-esteem: making positive changes by using his strengths and building a series of successes.

He started being more assertive and utilizing his strengths in two tough areas of his life: his job and his relationship with his mother. He thought through his work situation and went in and confronted his boss about a long overdue raise. He used his ability to organize facts and be diplomatic as he mapped out his strategy. He had carefully listed the strengths and capabilities he used on the job and detailed his progress and success. Much to his surprise, he got the raise.

This encouraged him to stand up to his mother and calmly yet persistently defend his and Lucia's decision to go to the beach that Christmas. Lucia almost went into a faint when she heard about this. Eric was further reinforced when Lucia actually initiated love-making that evening. Eric continued to build self-esteem and felt great about taking better control of his life. Things were on a positive roll as he *used* the gifts God had given him: gentleness, persistence and dependability, organizational skills, a deep sense of fairness, courage, and an understanding of people.

● TIME OUT _____

1. Talk through with your mate two areas in your life in which you need to mobilize your strengths, minimize your limitations, and take action. What particular strengths will you utilize? How will this boost your self-esteem?
2. Set up a goal/plan of action for accomplishing your two objectives.

---

4. Causes worth living for. A crucial part of escaping the blahs, becoming more self-assured, and enjoying selfness is reaching out beyond ourselves. In and of ourselves, we do not have meaning enough for life and happiness. We need God, human relationships, and causes worth living for. Our self-esteem is bolstered as we meaningfully and productively extend ourselves. It is a really positive cycle: the more we reach out, the more we feel good about ourselves; the more we feel good about ourselves, the more we reach out.

Haven't you seen this happen? As someone reaches out and helps their mate through school, they grow in their own self-confidence and find out so much about their own strengths. The depressed person who helps a newly bereaved widow suddenly gains perspective and an inner satisfaction that increases self-contentment and decreases depression. Focusing attention on children and extending ourselves for them gives us a satisfaction that makes us walk prouder and experience new things about our own selves. It is paradoxical but true that our self-concept and self-esteem will always be incomplete until we put something besides ourselves into the equation.

● TIME OUT _____

1. Can you list five causes worth living for? How do they impact your self-image and self-esteem? Which should you drop? What would be a helpful addition?
2. What part does your spiritual journey and relationship to God play in your causes?

_____

5. *Affirmation.* It is true that God's opinion of us is the focus, the central point, of our self-esteem and of knowing that we are each worthwhile and special. God also created us so that we crave and need human feedback. I have in my office a plastic cup given by a mental health center that lists 101 ways to praise a child. I sometimes read them off to myself and feel better. I really feel boosted when my wife or a friend uses some of them: "You're a joy. Nice work. You mean a lot to me. That's the best. Fantastic job. I knew you could do it. You made my day." Try repeating a few of these to those around you and ask for some in return. Feels great, doesn't it? What do you need to do to put yourself in a place of receiving more compliments? Give more.

Affirmation, compliments, praise, and feedback on our strengths and accomplishments are a vital part of our self-esteem and of loving companionship. The couples in chapters 1–5 all missed this part of their relationship. They doubted that they were lovable and began nitpicking rather than feeling secure. You know the vicious downhill cycle that ensued, with self-confidence battered and distancing setting in.

● **TIME OUT** _____

Write out a short newspaper advertisement selling your mate as The Fantastic Spouse. List all the strong points, personal charm, appeal, fantastic personality traits, as you help the readers understand how lucky they would be to have this person.

---

6. *Nurturing yourself.* Relaxation, exercise, doing things that bring a smile to your face, creating an adequate support network, enjoying being childlike and playful — all are important ingredients of self-nurture and help us feel good about ourselves. It is amazing how our leisure time activities like jogging, reading a book, or going to a concert help us to maintain perspective on life and to like ourselves, so that we can effectively reach out. Those tapes in my head of my own deep worthlessness and inadequacy run overtime when I am tired to the bone, when I have not taken the time to take care of myself. Playing tennis, watching a movie, hiking in the mountains, regular vacations, taking a bubble bath, a babysitting network are not optional items. A solid self-concept and great self-esteem are based on adequate self-nurture.

● **TIME OUT** _____

Make a list of thirty different things you enjoy doing to nurture yourself. Why are you neglecting so many? Do two this week!

---

7. *Healing the wounds and craziness.* Faye hated herself because she had bought all the negative messages her mom and ex-husband had told her over the years. "Your mouth is too

big. . . . You will never be able to do that. . . . Klutz, stupid, slow, fat, slut." Her present rage and resentment at her mom and ex made her less attractive and more down on herself. She was a great advertisement for this needed foundation stone for self-esteem—the need to forgive, erase negative messages, and heal the hurts. The walking wounded have a difficult time feeling self-esteem. As Faye engaged in God's redemptive process of confession, forgiveness, expressing feelings, and making changes, her self-concept slowly improved.

● **TIME OUT**————————————————————

1. Each of us at times needs to practice and experience the healing of harmful memories. Think of at least four important memories that still bring pain, anger, or guilt. Write them down in detail.
2. Now take them one at a time and pray over each, allowing Jesus to be there as you re-create the damaging scene in your mind and imagine Him forgiving and healing with a gentle word and touch.

IDENTITY

We call them many different things, from roles to identities to ego states to subpersonalities. Each of us has many parts to our personality. Our self-concept depends on working all of these into a happy and harmonious whole. Gil and Gretta were an interesting couple. At age forty-six, they were both in the midst of a full-blown, midlife identity crisis. They had just sent Jennifer off to college and Tommy was already married. Gil had just been passed over for a promotion, limiting his future with the large company he worked for; his bad knees were making him acutely aware of how he was aging. He was feeling a strong attraction to a twenty-six-year-old employee; he wondered whether he ultimately wanted to retire in the city or country.

Gretta missed her mom role and felt lost. She started back to school in special education and that helped, although being an older college student at first caused her misgivings.

She also took up painting and enjoyed creating landscapes. She joked with her best friend, Emily, that at some point she was going to have to decide what she wanted to be when she grew up. Over the past four years or so she had a heightened sexual desire and wondered if it were true that women gained their full sexual potential in their thirties and forties. She enjoyed the lake house, except that Gil was pretty moody and introspective these days, and not much fun when they went away. Thank God for her artwork, the boat, and other hobbies as well as her faith.

• UNDERSTANDING PERSONALITIES. Gil and Gretta are in the throes of doing what we all engage in over the course of our lifetime: sorting through and establishing a comfortable identity. You can observe in their lives how critical this process is for intimate companionship. We change over the years and this forces us to keep exploring and growing. One interesting school of psychology called Psychosynthesis states that each of us is made up of *subpersonalities* composed of needs, personality traits, and behaviors. These subpersonalities are important to understand, for they are more than the roles we play.

Gretta has a subpersonality that she labels "Nanny." This part of her needs to nurture and utilizes her patience and gentle caring. She used this in her role of mother and as a teacher of special education. Gil has an organizing executive subpersonality he calls "Boss." This was getting stymied at work, so he launched into creating a homeowner's association at the lake. Gil and Gretta are like so many couples who are struggling with identity: empty nest, lost promotion, needing a career track, forty years old, no children at home, sexual confusion, homemaker, harassed Christian, etc.

Identity struggles have a tremendous impact on our self-concept, marriage, and intimacy in general. Gil identified one of his subpersonalities as "Stud." He hastened to explain that this was much more than sexual and referred to his masculine attractiveness and his take-charge tendency — he was a magnificent stallion on the plains, tossing his mane and feeling greatly admired and respected. His career failure devastated this subpersonality and made him very vulnerable to the twenty-six-year-old's rapt attention and admiration.

• EXPLORING SUBPERSONALITIES. You probably have started thinking of yourself. What subpersonalities create your identity? Remember, a subpersonality is a deeper part of you than just a role you play (parent, club president). Many jobs you accomplish, like your career endeavors, utilize several of your subpersonalities; those separate parts of you that express important needs and personality traits, with behaviors appropriate to these needs and traits. Some of my counselees have named their subpersonalities: Clown, Dancer, Truckdriver, Audubon, Wimp, Preacher, Helper, Chief, Artsy, Comptroller.

Explore and understand at least five of your subpersonalities. A better self-concept increases your capacity for loving, supportive companionships. Get a pencil and have fun completing this exercise.

• **TIME OUT** _____

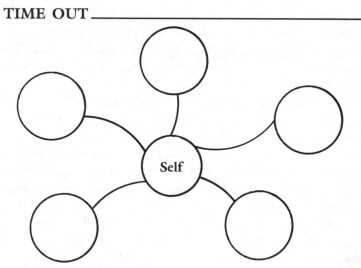

1. Relax in a quiet place and let your past week roll by you in review. Think of the different things you did and possible subpersonalities that were utilized. As subpersonalities slowly emerge, roll them around awhile in your mind as a name emerges. Write them in the circles.
2. Beside the circles, list the particular needs they express and the roles they play in your overall personality. When is each subpersonality most likely to be activated and how does it behave?

3. Reflect on each of your subpersonalities. What would happen if any one part controlled your life? What are its strong points? What unhealthy behaviors need to be kept under control?
4. Which parts are in conflict and how do you resolve this conflict? Which are allies?
5. Take each subpersonality again and think how you could accept and utilize it more fully. List two activities that would help fulfill that part of you.

I have a subpersonality I call Mentor, the part of me that loves to teach and patiently help people grow. It also is a bit of a show-off and enjoys attention. I have to be careful with it in my marriage, because my wife wants an equal companion, not a mentor—a simple answer not a lecture. Occasionally she will ask me to find something out, for instance to talk to a stockbroker about municipal funds. Then I may come home and teach and show off. I have to be careful because she has a Details subpersonality and after my report, she will have questions I never thought to ask. Now I go to such interviews with a list of questions made up by her Details. This is to sharpen up my Gentle Steamroller who obsessively gets jobs done but in an unassuming, intuitive manner, according to my priorities. This can drive my wife crazy, so I consult and allow parts of her to assist me. This keeps us both happier.

Gretta and Gil grew closer together as they understood themselves better. They helped each other fulfill personal needs and laughed a lot about their various subpersonalities and how they meshed or conflicted. Her Lover Girl fed right into his Stud; with some tune-up she was able to boost his ego and he loved her uninhibited love-making. They gradually got their act together and built a very satisfying individual and marital lifestyle. Their greater sense of identity boosted self-esteem and increased their ability to connect intimately.

Discuss the above section and exercise with your mate. Seek out new directions in work, leisure time, friendships, and spiritual commitments. I know you will find it satisfying to be more at peace with yourself and your mate as you build a unique lifestyle based on who you are as God's unique creation. Chapter 9 will continue your journey into self-awareness and identity, as you explore gender and personality styles and see how this can mesh with those of your mate.

CODEPENDENCE

Tom and Laura struggled in their marriage with trusting each other and their need to be in control. Because both were plagued by poor self-esteem and identity, and disappointed expectations, they engaged in wild, melodramatic fights. Their personal deficiencies were a great example of what is called *codependency*; together they created a crazy, codependent marital system. Codependency often evolves from dysfunction in our lives as children or from other traumatic events and losses. Codependent traits prevent couples from building the intimate companionship they desire.

In codependent marriages, conflict is used to distance rather than to resolve issues, and mates become enmeshed as they allow each other's mood to manipulate their own. They try to fix or take care of their partner rather than both working to become strong individuals. Remember, it takes two whole people to build a whole, intimate marriage. Think through your own traits and relationship patterns and evaluate how codependent you are.

● CODEPENDENT TRAITS.

1. Poor identity and self-esteem. Feeling worthless, fear of losing self, lack of self-awareness, cannot validate self, inability to define boundaries and be self-directive, caretaking and trying to make people like them.

2. Impostor phenomenon. "If someone truly knew me, they would not like me," dishonesty, isolation, secrecy.

3. Destructive feelings. Anger, guilt, shame, depression, and deep fears (of abandonment, being close) that are never resolved.

4. Revictimization. Vulnerability to destructive relationships, unrealistic expectations, inability to pick trustworthy people, repeating family mistakes.

5. Control needs. Excessive need to be perfect or have life under control, black-and-white rigid thinking; *or* impulsive, lack of healthy limits and procrastinating.

- CODEPENDENT RELATIONSHIPS.

1. Ineffective boundaries. Defensive walls that keep intimacy out *or* enmeshed relationships with unhealthy dependency, and desperate loyalty.

2. Trust deficits. Fear of abandonment, unresolved hurts, unrealistic expectations, and other codependent traits make openness and true bonding impossible. Possessiveness and defensiveness result in an inability to surrender control and trust.

3. Drama and illusions. Many angry and disappointed scenes with a lack of true identity, self-esteem, and strength. Two half people trying to create a whole relationship with tremendous mood swings, no consistency, and each partner manipulated by the other.

4. Closed system. A lack of outside input and poor support network, no openness to dynamic growth and healthy independence, enmeshed and rigid, very controlled.

CHANGING CODEPENDENT CRAZINESS

Healthy self-esteem and a secure identity strike a deadly blow against codependency. But there is another important step, one that seems paradoxical: taking control of life and letting go of control.

Tom discovered he exercised poor control over various areas of his life. His poor self-esteem propelled him into compulsive spending as he altered his mood and bolstered his ego by buying. He allowed his temper to go destructively unchecked and did not willfully seek to make any changes. He procrastinated even though he witnessed the severe damage being done by his lack of self-control in these areas. He wished he could mobilize and take charge.

In her perfectionism and fear of sexual feelings, Jenny could not relax her control in her early marriage. She feared losing control of her body and emotions and continually sabotaged a happy sexual companionship. Though it seemed strange to her, she began to work at being spontaneous and more playful. Jenny took charge by letting go of control, while Tom assumed more healthy control by carefully disciplining himself and his environment. Both were attacking codependency.

● MOBILIZING HEALTHY CONTROL. As he launched into taking control of his life, Tom found he had to balance two concepts: *insights* and *action*. The insights began with self-awareness of the problems, such as poor spending habits and no ideas of what a budget was. His insights then had to be taken a step further and a plan of action formulated. He tried to set careful goals with small, behavioral steps he could accomplish quickly. Tom decided on:

—putting all credit cards in the safe deposit box,

—balancing his checkbook weekly,

—seeing an accountant who would help him critique his spending and set up a simple budget.

Tom felt great about the insightful plan he had formulated, but Laura was skeptical because she knew her husband too well—he never followed through on ideas and goals. This time she was surprised because he mobilized his willpower and chose to take a series of actions that got him moving. He immediately scheduled an appointment with an accountant for the next week. He joined a men's group at the church primarily for accountability and better models for himself as a business person.

A couple of weeks into the group, he shared about his financial problems and the steps he was taking. One of the men encouraged him to take a vacation day from his job and lock himself in his office with his checkbook and financial records and truly get on top of things with eight hours of concentrated effort. Another wise person in the group asked him if he had written down any of the account numbers before putting the charge cards in the deposit box, so that he could still use them if he got in a pinch. Tom sheepishly said yes, and the man asked him to take the paper out of his wallet and destroy the numbers while he was watching.

Tom felt so much more in control of his life as he mobilized his willpower that Laura was amazed. A powerful, positive cycle was set in motion as he acted on his insights and continued to make changes. He also took further steps to increase accountability and avoid his personal sabotages. Tom was excited to finally be utilizing his mind and his will to revitalize his life and marriage.

● LETTING GO OF CONTROL. Jenny discovered that

she took control of her life and sexuality by letting go of control. She was plagued by perfectionism and an inability to live with loose ends and ambiguity in her life. She wanted everything structured and grew anxious when she couldn't control every aspect. There was a fear of spontaneity and playfulness or even of experiencing pleasure, because somehow it seemed too unpredictable and messy.

This affected her relationship to her children and her mate, and especially her sex life. Children have minds of their own and a house cannot stay orderly. Alex often did something new or unexpected. As she thought about their sex life, she slowly realized that to enjoy an orgasm she would need to allow excitement to take charge, relax control, and go with her feelings. Jenny started making equivalent changes in all areas of her life. She began to challenge her inner messages on neatness or her need to make everyone happy. She took little steps, like not dusting one end table or sensuously enjoying an unexpected ice cream cone. Gradually this all contributed to a less inhibited sexuality and a comfortableness with the unexpected. Ralph Waldo Emerson wrote, "A foolish consistency is the hobgoblin of little minds." We certainly want to rise above that as we take control of our lives.

As time went on, Alex and Jenny also worked at the other side of control. Jenny mobilized her willpower and refused further obligations that would make her life too busy. Alex relaxed his self-protectiveness and fear of intimacy. As he surrendered control, Jenny came closer and he reveled in the greater companionship.

SIX RESOURCES FOR PURSUING CHRISTIAN SELFNESS AND COUNTERING CODEPENDENCY

This could be the topic of a complete chapter but here are six suggestions to begin your journey toward wholeness. Your intimacy and marital happiness will rise only to the level of self-mastery you achieve in your life.

1. Counseling. So often Christians have a real stigma about going for counseling, yet God has gifted people to help others in this crucial area. Be a good consumer and choose someone who deals with your particular problem. Don't be afraid to find another counselor if the first one doesn't seem a good fit. Ask specific questions before going: "Are you a Christian? Do you work with sexual problems as a specialty? Would you feel comfortable exploring my anger toward God? Can you help me build self-esteem?" Use the Yellow Pages under psychologists, psychotherapy, or marriage and family therapists. Ask your minister. Realize that your problems were a long time in the making and may take at least six to eighteen months to heal. If you try it, I believe you will like it and wonder why you waited so long. You don't have to be on the brink of divorce to get assistance.

2. *Bibliotherapy.* This is a fancy word for reading books to find help for specific problems. I have included bibliographies in several of the chapters. This is an excellent way to gain insight and start to make changes. If you are a poor or unmotivated reader, get your mate to read the book and underline selective chapters. Books are great ways to combat and heal personal craziness.

3. *Groups.* This can be everything from self-help groups like Al-Anon or Codependency to a Sunday School class or a Bible study. Groups give us the opportunity to learn and to gain insight as we interact with others. We realize we are not alone, and we rub each other's rough edges off. You will only get as much as you are willing to contribute, so open up and share. Groups are a good way to grow and change.

4. *Workshops.* Many churches, community organizations, and educational institutions offer seminars and workshops on a variety of topics. These are excellent ways, on an evening or a Saturday, to learn new skills and develop your self-concept. It may be Dale Carnegie, or a creative conflict workshop, or assertiveness training. The class may necessitate some sacrifice of time and money, but a marriage enrichment retreat or another training course may be just what the doctor ordered.

5. *Pen and paper exercises.* There is a mystique about writing something down that makes it more concrete and impactful. Take the time to keep a journal as you sort through your thoughts. Make a budget with specific items. Write personal and marital goals. Go back and do some of the exercises in this book and other books as you make changes. Let's face it — we're lazy, and our personal craziness

does not change without a lot of work. Mobilize your will-power and start writing!

6. *Church.* Churches are marvelous places to find friends, gain practical insights, and learn more about God's economy for an abundant life. If we neglect spiritual growth, we have disregarded the foundation of intimate companionship. Church is like so many other aspects of life—we get back what we put into it.

FOR FURTHER READING

Robert Hemfelt, Frank Minirth, Paul Meier, *Love Is a Choice.* Nashville: Thomas Nelson Publishers, 1989.

Melody Beattie, *Codependent No More: How To Stop Controlling Others and Start Caring for Yourself.* Hazelden Foundation, San Francisco: Harper Collins, 1987.

Ruth Ward, *Self Esteem: Gift from God.* Grand Rapids: Baker Book House, 1984.

CHAPTER NINE

Celebrating Incompatibility

✠

*E*veryone is incompatible! I automatically make that assumption when counseling couples. We are each God's unique creation and in a variety of ways, totally different from each other. Three important categories that mates struggle with are *gender, style,* and *reality differences.* They are *male and female,* which goes much deeper than physiology. They each have a *personality style,* a unique way of interacting with the world. And they each have a unique family background, learning experiences, and genetic makeup which have created their *reality* of what the world truly is.

So many people fear that they have chosen the wrong mate and that incompatibility dooms their marriage. Rarely is this the case. Occasionally I will find a couple with deep value differences — Christian versus cult, do and don't want children — or individual scars and severe personality disorders which cannot be reconciled. Yet even in extreme cases, couples are often able to work out a comfortable companionship. Their incompatibility brings a richness to the relationship, and when understood and worked through, strengthens rather than damages the marriage.

GENDER DIFFERENCES

Jerry complained that his wife, Lisa, had a mind like a steel trap. She might forgive but she never forgot. It was never a simple, "I would appreciate you supporting me more when my parents criticize me." It was, "Do you remember the time when we first started dating in August of 1976? You came to pick me up for the school social and I came downstairs in my blue sleeveless dress and you had on that ugly brown suit. My dad told me the dress wasn't appropriate and you just stood there with your mouth shut and never said a word. It has been the same ever since." Jerry called it his wife's "pop-up file." She could recall every hurtful incident since they started dating and didn't hesitate to bring them up frequently when conflict occurred.

This is a fascinating gender difference. I commiserate daily with some frustrated husband who wonders how he can lay his past to rest. Sometimes he is angry because he cannot readily recall past incidents. I have pondered why women remember so well. Perhaps it is because they tend to use the right side (creative, visual part) of their brains more that visual images of incidents pop into their minds quite easily. Maybe it is a protective, maternal instinct which kicks in when they feel threatened, angry, or neglected. For whatever reasons wives do this, husbands get very frustrated and effective confrontation is sabotaged.

Jerry and Lisa followed a typical part of this pattern with Jerry responding to Lisa's recitation in an angry, attacking manner or sometimes, angrily withdrawing. Jerry was a master of fogging the issues with a forceful counterattack which would overwhelm Lisa. This would bring out more of her pop-up file and their interaction would disintegrate in anger and frustration.

As Jerry and Lisa learned to detach from their anger and fears and tried to understand each other's reality, they were able to make some changes. They took a quick course on the Psychology of Gender Differences as Lisa learned how threatening her tactics were to Jerry's male ego. He felt attacked and wondered if he could ever measure up to her expectations. His angry counterattacks stemmed from his insecurity and fear. With their present patterns her legitimate points were lost in the fog, as she became the nagging wife with a grudge.

She practiced sticking to the point and building up his self-respect with strategic compliments, along with her confrontation. She also brought out fewer past incidents from her pop-up file. To her amazement, Lisa found that Jerry was much less overwhelming and more willing to address issues as she changed her tactics. He was really a pussycat when he felt respected.

Jerry slowly realized that Lisa was actually quite forgiving, rather than being a grudge-holder. He discovered that she kept digging up old injustices and camping on his faults when she felt nothing was changing. As he began to be less angry, and more actively attended to her security needs, she did not resort to her steel trap memory. The past seemed to stay buried, the nagging stopped, and they actually resolved their conflicts.

Jerry and Lisa found that men and women have some very different needs and approaches to life. Lisa needed to feel secure. Jerry thought he was fulfilling that need by working hard and providing a home and amenities. That was not Lisa's definition of security. She was crawling the walls from lack of companionship and ached for emotional closeness. She wanted herself and her nest to be taken care of, and she could not understand how Jerry could stay overtime two hours at work to please a customer, but neglect some simple request of hers.

Jerry was mystified about why she got so angry when he neglected to check on life insurance or get the chimney leak fixed or initiate sex regularly. It started to fall into place better as he understood Lisa's needs and interpretation of security. He didn't mind risking less insurance or living with a leaky roof; Lisa was never a risk-taker when it came to her family or things that threatened her nest. He was comfortable with less connecting; she required emotional intimacy.

Lisa discovered that Jerry, like most men, got a lot of his ego strokes from what he did. He would sit and almost purr when she began telling him how proud she was of the job he did for the family. He was not being malicious when he neglected her security needs to earn approval at work. It was the way he was wired. She often thought of him as very passive and uninvolved or taking dumb chances, but now she wondered if part of it just wasn't a difference in priority. They argued for days over the second mortgage on the house. It made her feel very insecure, but somehow he knew he made enough to buy the house originally and the second mortgage would get paid off too.

Like many couples, they were each trying to comprehend a different gender reality. Lisa needed *security*, while Jerry needed to feel *respected*. Lisa's mind, when she felt threatened or tired of the lack of progress, could remember many incidents to back her case. Jerry's approach was a frontal assault or passive avoidance. Like so many men, he was inept in relational skills: feelings were a foreign language to him.

Jerry tried to be more self-disclosing as he opened up some of his hurt, love, and ambitions for Lisa to see. Though he was often fatigued and being physically demonstrative was tough, he practiced initiating hugs and gentle lovemaking. He could see how he came across in a threatening manner with his tirades, and he lowered the volume and intensity. He even started making lists of Lisa's priority requests and improved at recognizing her security needs. He saw that picking up the candelabra from her mother could wait, but the brakes on her car had better be checked today. Although some things did not seem that risky or important to him, he became more adept at nurturing and protecting, and at walking in Lisa's moccasins.

Though Lisa built Jerry up and tried to avoid a recitation of past mistakes, she had a tough time trusting him and allowing him to make changes. It seemed just when things felt secure, he would blow it again. She discovered an aggravating male characteristic of doing just enough changing to pacify her, but then a month later relapsing back into old behaviors. Lisa and I covenanted together to hold Jerry's feet to the fire long enough for permanent change to be enacted. She had to promise though that she would believe he could change and then keep her crazy desperateness in check. She did improve and that helped create more permanent change, but she still wondered why his male ego could be so fragile at times.

J.C. and Maribeth struggled with the gender gap too. He seemed to have a classic case of passive avoidance and male, left-brained analytical logic. Maribeth was so starved for a feeling or some means of connecting with J.C. that she felt like a wild, angry woman. A typical interchange would be:

Maribeth: "My boss is such a jerk!"

J.C.: "I think you need to either tell him off or get another job."

Maribeth: "My boss is a total idiot."

J.C.: "I've told you what I think."

Maribeth: "You never listen to me or care about what I feel."

From there it would disintegrate into their classic patterns of J.C. withdrawing in hurt anger while he wondered what he had done to deserve such a woman. Maribeth would follow him, trying to get some satisfactory connection, with her disrespect and disgust growing.

Maribeth didn't want J.C. to try to fix it, giving her two logical alternatives. She needed him to empathize with her feelings. Many a husband wonders what he has done wrong. He greets a distraught wife at the end of a hectic day at home with the children and she starts crying over how tired she is. He tries to help by suggesting that maybe she needs better time management and she hollers that maybe she needs a divorce. What Maribeth wanted was for J.C. to empathetically say, "You must be angry" or "That sure sounds like a tough situation," not to come back with logical alternatives.

I bluntly told J.C. that Maribeth would continue to sound like a broken record until he started dealing with her bottom-line need of having her feelings heard. When a husband tells me, "My wife won't shut up but keeps repeating herself" ("The kids are impossible, the kids are impossible"), he probably has not empathized with her feelings. Chances are he is being analytical or trying to fix it and needs to get out of the left hemisphere of his brain. His wife often just needs to be held. He can't fix everything.

The master marriage counselor Aaron Beck summarizes some common communication differences between husbands and wives. They certainly apply to J.C. and Maribeth. From childhood, women have a desire for intimate connecting and use talking to accomplish this. Feelings, secrets, and needs are expressed more easily by wives, while husbands tend to discuss less intimate topics like sports and business.

Women use questions as bridges to conversation and intimacy. Men take offense at this technique and feel they are being grilled. Husbands use questions more simply as requests for information. Wives want to problem-solve and talk things through as they connect and gain empathy and understanding. Their husbands don't want to discuss problems and feelings. They want to find practical solutions quickly.

In talking, women interrupt less and tend to want involvement. When interacting, wives will give little acknowledgments during a conversation, nodding the head or saying "Uh-huh." Husbands will interpret this as agreement rather than a technique of good listening. They are angry when their wives then take a different stance. Men stay silent during an interchange, then factually agree or disagree.

Maribeth learned to be more factual in her language. She quit resorting to crying in her confrontations and would formulate a list of reasons why her request was very logical and he would be foolish to ignore it. She hit him with language J.C. would understand. If the gutters do not get fixed:

– You will have to replace the wood around the porch,

– The basement will flood and your woodworking may get damaged,

– I will be very unhappy and believe me, you do not want that.

J.C. respected her approach and made much greater efforts, since she was less feeling-oriented and more logical. He also came to respect Maribeth for a certain intuitive grasp of situations that sliced through the fog much more quickly than his logic. She could read people and motives in a way he envied and came to rely upon. He began running some of his work situations by her and consequently got a better reading on his customers and colleagues.

Maribeth discovered a curious fact that men cannot do as many things at one time as women can. She made sure the ball game was off and the kids were in bed before she made her presentations. Otherwise, J.C. would not hear her. Her male boss was the same way: he couldn't chew gum and listen at the same time, so she kept things very focused. J.C. sometimes was angry but admitted he often did not hear her when there were any distractions. She could cook supper, tend the kids, and keep a conversation going at the same time, but he could not.

She appreciated his strength in leadership. She did not need him to try to make everything better, but she did enjoy his taking the initiative and being protective. She and J.C. discussed whether there was something God-given in maleness which needed to lead and what it meant for him to be head of their home as a Christian husband. J.C. seemed to thrive in taking the lead and Maribeth usually enjoyed this. She was a strong person and confronted him if he was being self-centered or domineering. This was a gender difference they worked smoothly into a comfortable respect and joint cooperation.

From Adam and Eve on, men and women have been trying to understand each other. With Jerry and Lisa, Maribeth and J.C., we have explored some of the common differences. I am not sure which of these are learned behaviors or God-given gender traits. Little boys are taught not to cry but to be strong; little girls are allowed a wider range of emotions. But this doesn't explain all. Johnny will come home after a morning playing trucks with Jimmy and say what a great time he had when the only communication was truck noises; Susy chatters all morning while having a tea party with Lucy.

Analytical and emotional skills, visual memory, leadership, security and respect needs, intuition—all can be the basis of a rich relationship. Of course we are taking for granted Adam and Eve want to get along better and that they are trying to grow in empathy, to compromise, and to try the wisest approach.

VARYING PERSONALITY STYLES

No two people interact with the world the same way and personality style can be a blessing or an aggravation. My wife tells me she could never sit hour after hour in the same chair in the same office; she is just too active for that. She appreciates my sedentary ability in helping people and in making a living for us, but this is not her style. I laugh and agree, for she does have to be up and about. This is the same wife who is upset with me on vacation because I want to read a book rather than be adventurous and hike an unknown trail. How do you win?

Each of us as individuals were born with and have devel-

oped a unique personality style. Couples are forced to struggle with this daily. Like any area of incompatibility, I have
found that the mate who understands his or her own style
and a mate's style, and *truly accepts this,* will negotiate and
compromise better. My wife, Catherine, does accept my
couch potato nature and appreciates that today I will sit
seven hours working on this book. She has also helped me
rub the rough edges off as I have discovered new facets of my
personality. I realize with hindsight that I have wasted a lot
of time watching football. I enjoy hiking and swimming
much more since being married to her.

Norm was more outgoing than Sandi, but they were not at
first aware of how deep their differences were. In dating days
Sandi's mom asked how she was enjoying being with such an
extrovert, since she was quiet and thoughtful. Sandi stated
she appreciated how Norm brought excitement and fun into
the relationship and made up for her shyness.

In the coming years they discovered so many ways the
introvert and extrovert differed. Norm liked to have noise
around and would immediately turn on the radio or television. She needed private, quiet time to think and regroup,
whereas he seemed energized by having people around.
Sandi pondered things in her head awhile before making a
statement, but Norm would think out loud, formulating as
he went. She was not always sure he meant what he said,
because he would make revisions constantly. His extroverted
style could be very confusing to her.

Some of this added a richness to their lives, but Norm let
certain of Sandi's personality traits deeply irritate him. He
became more aware of this after his affairs. He had come to
regard her as a real stick-in-the-mud, falsely judging her as
being antisocial and never able to have a good time. The
intimate New Year's Eve party with their two best couple
friends, and Sandi's enjoyment and laughter around
Pictionary, provided new insights. As they worked at restoring their sex life, he discovered she had more childlike curiosity and playfulness than he did. He began to accept and enjoy
her quiet nature more and realized his guilt during the affairs, not her actions or personality, had put Sandi in a
stodgy parental role.

A model of psychology called Transactional Analysis says that people have three parts or modes their personality operates from: Parent, Adult, Child.

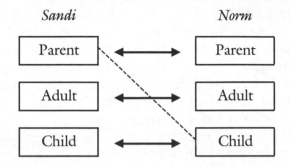

This is a fascinating model for couples to understand. Though people should be able to tune into their parent, adult, and child, T.A. says that a couple should try to never cross the transactions, but should stay parent to parent, adult to adult, child to child. The majority of a couple's communication should stay adult to adult; conflict can occur when this is violated.

This model helped Sandi and Norm work through some style differences. Sandi realized that just because Norm thought out loud or was more playful and impulsive, this did not mean he was always operating out of the child mode. Sandi was more introspective and thoughtful, but she sure did not want to be his mother. She got angry because she would start off what she hoped would be a solid adult to adult confrontation. In his guilt and insecurity, Norm lapsed into a little boy mode and would push her into a parental mode which she did not want. They worked hard at understanding each other's personality better and keeping the adults dominant. They both enjoyed the child mode sexually, when they were curious, excited, and uninhibited.

A personality style which easily falls into a parental mode is the Obsessive Organizer. Parker needed to have his world neatly pigeon-holed with no loose ends. His underwear had a precise spot in the middle of the drawer. He could put a hand on all the needed information within five minutes if his taxes ever got audited, and he stacked the dishwasher the same way every time. Unfortunately his wife, Tara, took a looser approach to life and had a fly-by-the-seat-of-your-pants style which drove him to distraction. Early in the marriage, he tried so hard to make her a carbon copy of himself that she felt completely stifled and angry.

Tara then began an almost adolescent rebellion as she left the house a mess, overspent, and let her relaxed style give new meaning to the phrase "hang loose." Both could see this wasn't working and that they needed to accept and respect each other more. They found, as so many couples do, that you are much more likely to accept and love your mates into changes than to nag or correct them into smoothing rough edges. These were tough incompatibilities to reconcile, even with love and acceptance.

Both learned to appreciate their mate to the point of adopting some of the best of the other's style. Tara found a certain amount of organization made life easier and more productive. Parker worked hard at a little spontaneity and less rigidness. He is still not laid back, but he allows himself to relax and every so often gets a little wild and crazy.

In some areas, they compromised by setting boundaries which prevented the styles from clashing. Parker promised not to redo what she had already done, especially loading the dishwasher, folding the linens, and adjusting the thermostat. She agreed that his desk and office were off-limits to her and the children. He would always drive if they went somewhere together. Parker could continue putting lists on the refrigerator, but she had the right to veto items or do the job in her style and speed. They each packed their own suitcases. He always had the go-ahead to take his own car if it looked like Tara was running late. This structure helped prevent many clashes.

A similar but tough area to reconcile was Tara's propensity to make decisions and operate through her feelings, since Parker was cerebral all the way. I may hasten to add that this is not necessarily a gender style issue. I always consult my wife, Cathy, on major decisions because she thinks with her head while I think with my heart. I will say, "Let's stay with that real estate agent; she is in a bad spot right now and it would help cheer her up." Cathy will reply, "Let's take her to lunch and encourage her, not risk thousands of dollars." Neither the thinking approach or feeling approach is always right or wrong.

Parker and Tara eventually came to rely on each other for a better perspective. They would discuss subjects like Christmas vacations and visiting their parents. Parker would practically state various logistics and time limitations. Tara would sort through diplomacy and gracefully deal with their parents' feelings. They evolved into a very effective team.

My mom is an optimist and my dad is a pessimist. After forty-seven great years of marriage, they still have this style difference. I chuckle when my mom calls and asks me to please talk to my dad. I know he must be on one of his pessimistic binges. It is amusing to me that most pessimists claim that they are actually realists. I recently saw a sign that said, "An optimist is someone who doesn't have all the facts." My mom will see the bright side and my dad as an introspective worrier will see the problems. Though he does forge ahead and accomplish much, it is more difficult for him to let go of negative events. Again, neither style is wrong but different, and couples like my parents compromise, adapt, and try to minimize the downside.

Most personality traits and styles of operating, like so many things in life, have a positive and a negative side to them. The introvert, the extrovert, the pessimist, the optimist, the feeler, the thinker, the active, the sedentary—all have to be polished or they can become lazy, rigid, immobilized, domineering, unrealistic, passive, insensitive. Sometimes a style is simply learned craziness and needs to be altered for marital intimacy to thrive. Parker changed some of his obsessive demandingness while Tara tightened up her messiness. Norm tempered his impulsiveness, and Sandi let her child out. Styles truly differ but they can be blended, adapted, kept separate, maximized, or changed as intimacy thrives.

UNIQUE REALITIES

Have you ever carefully explained ten logical reasons why your point of view is correct, only to have your mate remain unconvinced? Sometimes marriages remind me of our softball games when I was a boy. The games took place in a vacant lot between two houses. We made up our own ground rules — the orange tree in right field was a double, the street was a home run, and three foul balls and you were out. One day after not playing for a week, I hit a double into Mr. Johnson's yard. The group all said, "You're out." I argued that it was a double and they stated that the rules had been changed since Johnny put a ball through Mr. Johnson's window. Everything in his yard was now an out. This is the way so many people feel in marriage. They are playing a game and then find their mate has a different set of rules. It is difficult to know when they have hit a home run or struck out.

The most difficult task I have as a marriage counselor is to help each partner walk in their mate's moccasins and try to understand their reality. Remember the unrealistic expectation we explored in chapter 7 — "My mate will be similar to me in values, thinking, and needs"? We are each unique creations, as has already been demonstrated with gender and style. In addition to being male or female, possessing a distinct mode of operating, our mates come to us from their own family background and have gone through many pleasant and unpleasant experiences which have shaped their view of reality. We have to somehow take our glasses off and put theirs on if we are ever going to understand and overcome this *reality* incompatibility.

Remember Tom and Laura who had experienced life so differently? Tom was the youngest child whose sick brother Jimmy consumed so much of his mother's time and whose dad had a problem with alcohol. Tom learned to be alone and amuse himself; he would defend himself with protective temper outbursts when needed. Laura had a loving father who worked a lot during high school years. A short-lived marriage left her with daughter, Tiffany, and financial nightmares. Her security needs had quadrupled by the time Tom met her, but at least she was more aware than he was of how a healthy family operated. Their realities and expectations of each other were drastically different.

Using a Venn diagram will help us understand how Tom and Laura were real mysteries to each other.

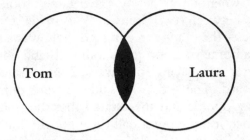

The shaded part of the diagram is that which they understood about each other. You can see that they related with little understanding of the other's rules and reality. The next diagram demonstrates that God has *a reality, an economy for relationships.* In His economy we heal our scars, get rid of unrealistic expectations, and learn to truly be honest and loving as we create deep intimacy. With her healthier family background and the support of her discerning friend Evie, Laura is more congruent with God's reality than is Tom.

We can superimpose the circles of God's, Tom's, and Laura's reality. The shaded area shows the degree to which Tom and Laura understand each other's reality and are congruent with God's economy. In their beginning relationship this was quite small. The barred area is the part of Tom and Laura's reality they are aware of each other but both could use some changes as they adopt God's economy. As time went on and they wanted to make changes, they were able to help each other rub off rough edges in this barred area, as they grew more congruent with God's reality.

The goal in building great companionship and dealing with incompatibility is really quite simple: *making the circles more congruent* and increasing the shaded area. Tom is striving to understand Laura's needs, scars and hot buttons, personality style, gender differences, her language, and what symbolizes security to her—to truly walk in her moccasins and comprehend her reality. Laura is trying to do the same with Tom.

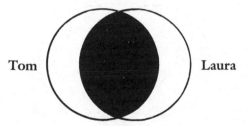

Tom and Laura are not trying to agree or be similar to each other's reality. They are working at *understanding* the other and strengthening their ability to function intimately together. Even as they conform more and more to God's economy for intimate relationships and adopt His will and way with greater love and honesty, they still will have their *unique differences*. Tom can learn self-awareness and discipline (God's reality), but he will always spend money more freely than Laura. Laura can heal the scars of her ex-husband's abuse and learn to trust Tom (God's economy), but she will always be more cautious.

They both realize it will be a lifelong process of learning to understand each other and conform to God's economy. The fruit of the Spirit is love, joy, peace, patience, kindness, goodness, faithfulness, gentleness and self-control" (Galatians 5:22).

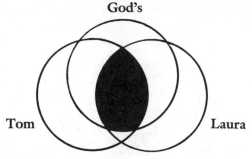

CREATING A DYNAMIC RELATIONSHIP
There are some practical steps Laura and Tom and other couples can follow in learning each other's and God's reality. They are traits intimate couples have to practice as they work through all forms of incompatibility (gender, styles, etc.) and create a dynamic companionship.

1. Be humble. I have been deeply touched recently by the concept of humility. Anytime I feel I have a corner on truth and rigidly bull ahead, I miss out on a wiser and better course of action God had for me. I often insensitively hurt those I love the most and end up a poorer mate or psychologist. Proverbs 11:2 states it eloquently, "When pride comes, then comes disgrace, but with humility comes wisdom." All the couples in this chapter had to step back and humbly acknowledge that their mate's differences were normal and okay. They did not have a direct line to God's truth or *the* correct way of functioning. Each gained flexibility, helpful insights, and deeper appreciation of their mate, as they humbly stepped back from themselves and tried to comprehend a different reality.

2. Be inquisitive and detached. Good mates are great detectives! They detach from the situation and their own perceptions and try to find out what is really happening. They curiously explore the incompatible, mysterious parts of the puzzle. They try to understand motives and how the other person thinks and what their language symbolizes. What does it mean when they say, "You are just like your mom/dad. I hate the beach. Sex is in a rut. I am unhappy." They inquisitively go to some codependency meetings, learn and practice some Italian if that is what their mate's family speaks, question the relatives and assertively risk looking foolish as they gain information. They don't jump to conclusions, but flexibly consider solutions they did not think possible at first.

3. Be patient. I am trying to find a way to say something very commonplace right now and yet have you the reader perk up and say, "Wow, that is profound!" Here it goes, *"Everything takes time."* Now it is your turn, "Wow!" The aggravating truth about incompatibility is that it will take a long period of time and much energy to work through it. When couples come to me, especially those who are in the courtship process, and say, "We have a great relationship but fight a lot over her need to have everything carefully organized," I know there is no simple answer. With patience and work, they do not have to jeopardize their intimacy. Friends always tell me to be careful when I pray for patience—it can be a painful virtue to learn. But patience and time are invaluable in working through differences.

4. Be positive. You love and accept people into changes. Negative nagging, hollering, avoidance, discouragement, muckraking are very ineffective. Lisa had to grow a positive attitude that Jerry could and wanted to change. At first she had to mobilize her willpower and behave more positively before a more positive attitude would come. It is normal that a couple's differences will create hurt, anger, disappointment, and doubt that the marriage can work. This is where our relationship with God is important, as we allow His strength to be there for us. He can help us poke holes in our backpack of resentments, hurt, and craziness. He can help us gear our minds to the peace and joy we need—to effect changes and live happily ever after.

5. *Be active.* The Serenity Prayer encourages, "God grant me the Serenity to accept the things I cannot change, Courage to change the things I can, and Wisdom to know the difference." Mates who want great marriages have to be action-oriented, accepting incompatibilities that cannot be changed and learning to enjoy or minimize them. Parker came to appreciate some of Tara's hang-loose approach to life and encouraged her to assume responsibility in areas where his rigidity would just get in the way. They also agreed for Tara and the children to stay out of his office, as they minimized conflict and kept her mess out.

All the couples whose relationships we explored in this chapter discovered traits they needed to change. They actively sought to rub off the rough edges of their differences and create compromise where each one's needs were met. As they slowly accepted or made changes, the incompatibilities took less of a toll and actually added variety and strength to their intimate companionship.

FOR FURTHER READING

Chuck and Barb Snyder, *Incompatibility: Grounds for a Great Marriage.* Sisters, Oregon: Questar Publishers, Inc., 1988.

CHAPTER TEN

Easy to Learn Communication Skills

✠

$\mathcal{M}$y wife sometimes complains, "You aren't listening." I immediately bristle, because I hate criticism and get defensive so easily, and because I make my living listening. There are many things I cannot do well, but I consider myself a professional listener. Yet, the more I think about her complaint, I grudgingly acknowledge she is right. I wasn't listening to her, but was preoccupied with a problem at work or the television. It is so easy to lapse into poor communication skills, even if you make a living at listening. This chapter will develop the three important parts of communication.

Sender ◀━━━━━▶ Message ◀━━━━━▶ Listener

Under each of these three areas, we will explore four principles that are vital to being an effective sender or listener of messages. The final section of this chapter will deal specifically with confrontation and conflict, a necessary and crucial part of intimate communication.

After one counseling session, I was amused when my client told me, "You didn't tell me nothing my mama hasn't already told me." I replied that that was probably true and if he were practicing what his mama had said, he would not be in my office. You may feel like this client as you study these communication skills. Many of them are commonsense things you know to do but neglect. I hope these explanations will make them easier to understand and apply.

COMMUNICATION SKILLS

A. THE PROFESSIONAL LISTENER

1. **Focused Listening** Eye contact, eliminate distractions, memory concentration, message acknowledgment.
2. **Detached Listening** Personal judgments suspended, hot spots improved, no overpersonalizing/projection, avoid rebuttals.
3. **Empathetic Listening** Walking in their moccasins, understanding another's reality, unconditional acceptance, respect.
4. **Accurate Listening** No assumptions or mind reading; clarify ("Do you mean . . . " What vs. Why?), active listening with feedback.

B. THE ACCOMPLISHED SENDER

1. **Self-awareness & Security** Self-esteem; awareness of feelings, strengths and limitations; self-disclosing; practicing Serenity Prayer as rough edges rubbed off.
2. **Using "I" Language** Taking personal responsibility, not blaming "you" language with judgments.
3. **Assertiveness** Openly express needs/feelings/desires, risk conflict, not aggressive or passive, no hinting (*honest* statements—not questions) or fragile tiptoeing or gunnysacking of feelings.
4. **Dialogue** (not debate) Seek information and solutions—not wins; loving and humble process; respectful, flexible, not defensive.

C. EFFECTIVE MESSAGES

1. **One-track Is Better** Stick to one topic and finish the message; avoid changing to comfortable topic or handling three topics at the same time or muckraking.
2. **Needs & Feelings Are Bottom Line** Cut to the core and define deeper issues (needs and feelings); don't debate, lecture, rehash, deal in personalities and details.
3. **Develop Effective Timing** Be strategic, not hungry or angry, but don't avoid or gunnysack.
4. **Positive Communication Works** Eliminate "never, always, won't/don't"; no below the belt or power plays; keep the volume down; no scorekeeping; no withdrawing.

THE PROFESSIONAL LISTENER

The Bible states that we "should be quick to listen, slow to speak and slow to become angry" (James 1:19). The listening part of communication is the one that so often breaks down; then intimacy is slowly destroyed, as we observed with Jerry and Lisa in chapter 5. I tell my clients that if they want a great marriage, they will have to become professional listeners. This means learning four dynamic skills every professional listener has had to master.

1. Focused listening. When my wife tells me I am not listening to her, this is the skill I am usually neglecting. Men especially have trouble with this skill as they watch a ball game or ponder a problem from work while they try to listen. This doesn't work. I think God has blessed women with a greater ability to do two things at once. My wife can cook and listen, pay partial attention to our daughter, and yet hear me. I can't. I think men especially need to keep on one track and eliminate distractions to be a good listener.

I have realized after some major conflict that to be a focused listener at home, I have to re-create my office atmosphere and skills. I *eliminate distractions* by turning off the television or stopping a minute what I am doing. I try to position myself across from the speaker and maintain *eye contact* as I pick up nonverbal as well as verbal messages. I once heard a lecturer claim that 90 percent or more of all communication is nonverbal. I also *concentrate my memory* as I focus my attention on what is being said both to hear it and remember it for use now and in the future. I am *not* focusing my memory on my rebuttal but simply on taking in and truly hearing. Finally, I *acknowledge* that the message is being received. This may be by nodding my head or saying "Uh-huh" or "I'm hearing you." This acknowledgment reassures my partner I am listening carefully. *Practicing with your mate is the only way to learn!*

● TIME OUT

1. Pick a topic of conversation and both practice arranging the environment and your mental processes to truly listen well. Cut out all distractions, sit face-to-face, and focus your memory and attention as you acknowledge the other.

Does this help? How is it different from what you usually
do?
2. Sit face-to-face and pick a topic. Use a timer and let the
   first person talk three minutes. Now the listener has to
   summarize back exactly what he or she heard until the
   mate agrees that he or she heard accurately. Reverse positions and keep practicing.

---

2. Detached listening. Often we do not hear a message because we are preparing our defense while the other person is
talking. This makes for very poor listening. Recently I
jumped in with a defense, only to have my friend say, "Did
you hear the last thing I just said?" I had to apologize, for
indeed I had not and didn't even need the rebuttal. Good
listeners *detach* from their own issues, feelings, and thinking
while they focus on the message.

It is not easy to detach and *put on hold* our own judgments
and feelings, especially certain emotionally loaded issues.
That is why it is crucial for good listeners to *clean up their
own hot spots.* Lisa and Jerry were both so afraid he would
become like his dad that this topic became very touchy. Jerry
tried to better understand and accept his dad. As he began
making changes in areas he did not want to be similar to his
father, he found he could detach to hear messages from Lisa
without *overpersonalizing* and taking major offense. Lisa had
to come to grips with her fears, not only about Jerry's dad
but also her own father, before she could distance enough
not to *overreact or project* Jerry onto his dad. Now they both
can detach enough to talk objectively and hear each other's
messages about parents and behaviors they do not want to
repeat.

Jerry and Lisa also learned the importance of *respect* in
detaching. They did not have to agree with or accept what
the other said, but they did need to detach enough to respect
the right of the other person to have an opinion. In listening,
their goal wasn't to agree but to suspend their hostility, disgust, or fear, so that the other person was given the privilege
of being heard—not an easy task but one that improved with
practice.

● TIME OUT —————————————————————————

1. Pick a loaded topic in your relationship; this time do not discuss the topic but dissect why it is such a hot spot. Be a detective. Explore why you have such strong feelings, why you take it so personally, why you get defensive. What is the history of this topic, going clear back to childhood?
2. Now discuss this topic with your partner as each of you consciously tries to detach and suspend personal feelings and judgments while you listen. Was it better?

———————————————————————————————

3. Empathetic listening. There is a saying that you should never criticize someone until you have *walked a mile in his moccasins.* Empathizing and truly understanding *another person's reality* is one of the most difficult and yet important listening and communication skills. Paul and Patsy struggled with understanding each other's sexual reality. Paul was concerned that their sex life had fallen into a rut and he tried to put some spark back into it. He started modeling behaviors for Patsy that he knew would increase his own sexual desire and enjoyment: walking around nude, buying Patsy some sheer lingerie, and talking about sexual activities that could be fun to try. These behaviors made Patsy pull back even more. She tried to tell Paul that she saw him the most sexy in his red gym shorts and that she wished they could minimize the effects of the kids and get away for a quiet, romantic weekend.

Everything Patsy said was filtered through Paul's reality. He was hurt that she didn't see and hear the efforts he was making. Paul was trying to hear Patsy's French through his German ears and missing all her key points. For her, nudity and varied sexual activity was not as arousing as Paul partially clothed, and their being together in a romantic, relaxed atmosphere. A professional listener has the ability to get into another person's mind and reality and understand his language; otherwise, feelings are hurt and the message is heard as an undecipherable code. This inability to empathize landed Paul and Patsy in my office where we worked through better relational and empathy skills. The sex then took care of itself.

The skill of empathy and listening carefully in an intimate relationship depends on *unconditional love and respect.* The Bible tells husbands, "Be considerate as you live with your wives and treat them with respect" (1 Peter 3:7). Another translation is, "Live according to knowledge." True love is based on knowledge and an empathetic understanding of your partner's reality. Your mate won't feel heard if you don't love and respect his or her needs, feelings, and opinions. Empathetic listening helps you forget about yourself and about winning points as you lovingly try to understand and truly hear your companion's reality.

● TIME OUT_____

1. Ask your mate what is sexy to him or her; detach as you empathetically and lovingly get inside their reality. Are you hearing some new things? What do each of you need to implement?
2. Pick one topic on which you disagree. One of you discuss his or her views, needs, feelings on the first topic and then leave the subject with *no* rebuttal. Now the other will take the second topic and repeat the process with only empathetic listening and no response. Discuss how you feel afterward.

_____

4. Accurate listening. Paul thought he knew how Patsy felt, because of the way *he* thought and felt. A key factor in professional listening is to *never assume or mind read; check it out, clarify,* and get *feedback.* So often in my practice someone will use a word or make a statement that I think I understand; but when I check it out, I find they meant something entirely different. Someone will say, "I hate him," which can mean everything from, "I'm frustrated," to, "I love him to death but hate it when he is always late," to, "I have made active plans to kill him."

As a professional listener I use phrases like, "Run it by me again," "Do you mean. . . ?" "Here is what I heard you say . . . " "You feel. . . . Am I on target?" I ask *what* questions and not *why.* A mate often asks, "Why do you feel that way?"

or, "Why do you think that way?" The point is that they *do* feel or think that way. The effective listener is *detached* and *empathetic* and asks *clarifying What* questions. "What else are you feeling?" "Help me understand better what is going on with you." Paul finally clarified what was sexually stimulating to Patsy and their lovemaking got back on track.

● TIME OUT

1. Practice having your mate make a statement and then you reply with three "Do you mean . . . " statements and see if you can get two out of three correct. E.g., Do you mean my manners are poor? Yes. Do you mean you're embarrassed when I scratch myself in public? Yes. Etc. Etc.
2. Brainstorm together to come up with several ways you could clarify messages and maintain accuracy. Try them out.

We should be quick to listen and slow to speak. The professional listener knows how to focus in, detach from feelings and judgments, work on hot spots, empathize and understand a foreign reality, and never assume or mind read but clarify. Commonsense skills, but they work!

THE ACCOMPLISHED SENDER

Becoming an excellent Christian communicator means growing as a person and becoming more Christlike. It means valuing honesty, learning to love, becoming secure with true self-respect, taking responsibility, and eliminating defensiveness. This is especially obvious as we discuss how to become an accomplished sender of messages.

1. Self-awareness and security. "Buy the truth and do not sell it; get wisdom, discipline and understanding." "A wise man's heart guides his mouth" (Proverbs 23:23; 16:23). It is difficult communicating with our partner if we do not *understand ourselves.* It is difficult risking self-disclosure if we don't feel *secure* about our self-concept. Harry was in my office after a huge fight with his wife, P.J. All he could explain was it started because he felt "bad." It became obvious that until

COMMUNICATION SKILLS

A. THE PROFESSIONAL LISTENER

1. **Focused Listening** Eye contact, eliminate distractions, memory concentration, message acknowledgment.
2. **Detached Listening** Personal judgments suspended, hot spots improved, no overpersonalizing/projection, avoid rebuttals.
3. **Empathetic Listening** Walking in their moccasins, understanding another's reality, unconditional acceptance, respect.
4. **Accurate Listening** No assumptions or mind reading; clarify ("Do you mean . . . " What vs. Why?), active listening with feedback.

B. THE ACCOMPLISHED SENDER

1. **Self-awareness & Security** Self-esteem; awareness of feelings, strengths and limitations; self-disclosing; practicing Serenity Prayer as rough edges rubbed off.
2. **Using "I" Language** Taking personal responsibility, not blaming "you" language with judgments.
3. **Assertiveness** Openly express needs/feelings/desires, risk conflict, not aggressive or passive, no hinting (*honest* statements — not questions) or fragile tiptoeing or gunnysacking of feelings.
4. **Dialogue** (not debate) Seek information and solutions — not wins; loving and humble process; respectful, flexible, not defensive.

C. EFFECTIVE MESSAGES

1. **One-track Is Better** Stick to one topic and finish the message; avoid changing to comfortable topic or handling three topics at the same time or muckraking.
2. **Needs & Feelings Are Bottom Line** Cut to the core and define deeper issues (needs and feelings); don't debate, lecture, rehash, deal in personalities and details.
3. **Develop Effective Timing** Be strategic, not hungry or angry, but don't avoid or gunnysack.
4. **Positive Communication Works** Eliminate "never, always, won't/don't"; no below the belt or power plays; keep the volume down; no scorekeeping; no withdrawing.

Harry learned more about his feelings, he would never send effective messages. I asked what he felt bad about and did he feel bad/irritated or bad/disappointed? After careful exploring, we concluded he had felt angry/put-down because P.J. had questioned his judgment about wanting to build a deck on the house. He was notorious for never finishing projects, and in his insecurity and anger lashed out at her the next day about some minor point. Harry began a crash course on feelings and increasing his *self-esteem*. He learned to appreciate his *strengths* and shore up his *weaknesses*.

P.J. wasn't aware that her messages were delivered in a condescending tone which drove Harry wild. As we explored that, it came out she was afraid Harry would never change and she was stuck with a mate with a lot of flaws. As she became more self-directed and in tune with her feelings, she was able to send better messages. As Harry grew and changed with greater confidence and understanding of himself, he disclosed more of himself and she felt more included.

Though self-awareness and self-esteem may seem odd to include as important principles for effective communication, they are bottom line. Harry and P.J. were stuck until they learned more about themselves and were able to rest securely in who they were as people. They could then accurately send messages and securely forget about themselves as they reached out and truly connected with each other.

● TIME OUT

1. List ten things you truly like about yourself and five things you observe as weaknesses which need to be minimized or perhaps changed. Remember, our strengths often include our weaknesses: a strong personality may be a bulldozer.
2. Relate to your mate the three situations in life that make you feel the most insecure. Discuss how to deal with them.

---

2. *"I" Language.* Most books on communication say that an accomplished sender should use "I" language. Using "I"

language means taking responsibility for your feelings by keeping them in the first person. "*I* am angry when you are late and think you don't value my time," rather than, "*You* are a super jerk; you're always late and you make me so angry." Blaming "you" statements make the person you are communicating with so defensive that you can almost see the fur on his back start to rise as he gets ready to lash back. It is more honest for you to claim responsibility for your personal thoughts and feelings.

Tom knew that Laura froze up or lashed out when he attacked her in the second (you) or third person (she) but then again Tom often thought, "She can be such a nag, and too, she utilizes the same lousy communication patterns I do." There he was again, using the third person, a tough habit to break. In therapy I would call Tom and Laura on this and make them restate their sentences using the first person. "I get frustrated, Laura, when I think you are lecturing me and yet engaging in the same mistakes." "Tom, I am scared and angry whenever I am reminded of my ex-husband."

Tom and Laura learned to be less judgmental and more in control of their own lives as they made "I" statements. They realized that the other person did not create the fear or anger, as in "*You* make me frustrated." Their feelings were their own personal reactions which they handled as they chose: either with blaming "you" statements or with nondefensive, responsible "I" statements. It did not come easily and they relapsed occasionally, but they learned that "I" statements were much more effective.

● TIME OUT _____

1. Take an emotionally loaded topic and each of you stick to "I" statements, especially trying to express your feelings.
2. Relapse into "you" statements and analyze how it increases defensiveness and is judgmental, blaming, and dishonest.

---

3. *Assertiveness.* This is an important principle of commu-

nication, and of becoming an accomplished sender of messages, that many people struggle with. What we should be able to do is give our messages in a *straightforward, nonaggressive,* and *confident* manner. What we actually do is quite different.

Which of the following ineffective, *nonassertive techniques* are you guilty of?

– Hinting. This is when you beat around the bush rather than say what you feel or need. Often, it is done with a question, "Do you feel upset about that?" rather than, "That irritates me to no end." Or, sometimes a series of questions, "Do you feel hungry?" "Can we afford to go out tonight?" "What do you think of Chinese?" instead of, "I would love to eat Chinese tonight. Can we afford to go out?"

– Avoiding conflict and rejection. This is related to hinting. Most people are not masochists who want to seek out pain and rejection, but conflict and pain are a normal part of intimate relating. We are each unique male and female individuals and we will feel, need and desire different things. This uniqueness creates differences with conflict and rejection. Assertive persons accept this and persist in expressing their feelings. They know their needs won't always be met and that is okay. They are confident that conflict and confrontation can effectively lead to resolution or some compromise.

– Aggressiveness. Assertiveness training courses try to distinguish between passive (avoiding or coming in the back door with hinting or sarcasm), assertive, and aggressive behavior. Aggressive communication tries to win and overwhelm people rather than to dialogue and negotiate. It shuts down the intimate connecting that is the true purpose of messages.

– Fragile tiptoeing. When we walk on eggs around our partner, both of us have lost an essential ingredient of assertive communication. Sometimes this happens because one or both partners create the aura of being fragile in a given area: "If you talk about my mother, I will cry," or "Mention sex and I will be devastated." Great message senders toughen up, don't tiptoe, and assertively confront all areas of the relationship.

– Gunnysacking. This is related to tiptoeing but includes storing up feelings or experiences and refusing to express them. We stuff them in our gunnysack until it explodes and they come pouring out in a destructive way.

Remember, assertiveness in communication means openly expressing your thoughts, feelings, needs, and desires in a confident, persistent, and positive manner. "I" statements are good examples. In expressing feelings it is important to stay with adjectives that describe your feelings. Otherwise, you may be expressing a thought or opinion and not a feeling. In trying to learn to express feelings, one of my clients told his wife, "I feel that you are stupid sometimes." I hastened to tell him that this wasn't a feeling; he was actually saying, "I *think* you are stupid."

● TIME OUT

1. Discuss with your mate which of the ineffective techniques each is most guilty of. How could you try different behaviors? Practice one right now.
2. Think about your own assertiveness level and decide which of the following scenarios would be difficult: asking a waitress to move you after you are already seated; telling your parents you do not agree with what they said; confronting your mate when you know conflict will erupt; asking for something when you know you probably will be refused.

---

4. Dialogue. This is a critical concept in sending and receiving messages, especially in a conflict situation. The goal of communication is to *gather and send information* and *seek solutions, not wins.* It is a *humble* and *loving* process in which people are able to reach out beyond themselves and admit they don't have a corner on truth and can empathetically put another person's needs ahead of their own. It is *flexible* and nondefensively *negotiating* and *compromising.*

Accomplished senders dialogue as they *send and receive data.* They do not try to win, make judgments, assume or mind read, overwhelm or belittle; rather, they create and foster a mutual dialogue. Dialogue utilizes all of the listening and sending skills we have talked about so far. A great dialoguer is both a professional listener (focused, detached, empathetic, informed) and an accomplished sender (self-aware/secure, responsible, assertive). When you need to confront, keep reminding yourself that communication is dialogue, dialogue and data, dialogue and solutions, dialogue and feelings, dialogue, dialogue! I am secure; I am responsible; I am assertive. I can dialogue.

● TIME OUT _____

1. Choose a sticky family problem (parents, brother-in-law, holidays) that the two of you have never agreed on. This time you are going to reverse roles with your partner and take the opposite viewpoint, as you pretend what you used to believe is all wrong and your mate's position is right. Dialogue about the situation from these reversed roles to better get in touch with the whole spirit of dialogue.
2. Take the subject of your most recent fight, only this time send messages in a dialogue manner. Forget about winning or convincing; both of you simply send and collect data as you try to develop a true understanding of the situation.

EFFECTIVE MESSAGES

You are probably feeling overwhelmed with communication principles by now. Remember they are common sense; most of them you already know and understand, but you just don't practice them. This is certainly true of the four characteristics of an effective message: one-track, bottom line, well-timed, and positive.

1. One-track. A good message sticks to the topic until it is completed. When Norm was involved in and feeling guilty about his affair, he constantly violated this principle whenever Sandi confronted him about his neglectful behaviors. Because he knew he was wrong, he would change the topic to one of her shortcomings. Sandi would then get defensive and

COMMUNICATION SKILLS

A. THE PROFESSIONAL LISTENER

1. **Focused Listening** Eye contact, eliminate distractions, memory concentration, message acknowledgment.
2. **Detached Listening** Personal judgments suspended, hot spots improved, no overpersonalizing/projection, avoid rebuttals.
3. **Empathetic Listening** Walking in their moccasins, understanding another's reality, unconditional acceptance, respect.
4. **Accurate Listening** No assumptions or mind reading; clarify ("Do you mean . . . " What vs. Why?), active listening with feedback.

B. THE ACCOMPLISHED SENDER

1. **Self-awareness & Security** Self-esteem; awareness of feelings, strengths and limitations; self-disclosing; practicing Serenity Prayer as rough edges rubbed off.
2. **Using "I" Language** Taking personal responsibility, not blaming "you" language with judgments.
3. **Assertiveness** Openly express needs/feelings/desires, risk conflict, not aggressive or passive, no hinting (*honest* statements — not questions) or fragile tiptoeing or gunnysacking of feelings.
4. **Dialogue** (not debate) Seek information and solutions — not wins; loving and humble process; respectful, flexible, not defensive.

C. EFFECTIVE MESSAGES

1. **One-track Is Better** Stick to one topic and finish the message; avoid changing to comfortable topic or handling three topics at the same time or muckraking.
2. **Needs & Feelings Are Bottom Line** Cut to the core and define deeper issues (needs and feelings); don't debate, lecture, rehash, deal in personalities and details.
3. **Develop Effective Timing** Be strategic, not hungry or angry, but don't avoid or gunnysack.
4. **Positive Communication Works** Eliminate "never, always, won't/don't"; no below the belt or power plays; keep the volume down; no scorekeeping; no withdrawing.

lash back. The original topic and whole reason for the confrontation would be lost; all the muck of past fights would be raked up and Sandi would become the goat.

When this occurs in a counseling session, I point out what is happening. A wife was confronting her mate about his going into the office both Saturday and Sunday. He made a quick rebuttal but sensed he was losing, and so jumped her about a speeding ticket; she got angry and remembered last night when she had gotten up to go to the bathroom and had sat on cold porcelain because he had left the toilet seat up. I intervened before it could degenerate further.

Sometimes messages get offtrack, not as an avoidance technique, but because one topic will suggest another until all of a sudden you are *balancing four topics* in the air. I will sometimes say in a session, "That is a good topic and needs to be dealt with. Let's get to it next after we have finished this one." Mom's visit will trigger the need for a new mattress which will trigger Susy's request for a new bed for her birthday which will trigger Susy's messy bedroom, and all of a sudden there are four messages being dealt with and none resolved. One-track communication is better.

● TIME OUT

1. Play with the one-track concept. With your partner, deliberately try to change the topic or get four going at once. Discuss how frustrating and unwieldy this becomes. How did each of you feel?
2. Try this exercise again, only this time one of you will be designated to keep things on track. Then switch roles.

---

2. Bottom-line. So often couples stay very superficial as they *nitpick*, endlessly *debate, rehash* old arguments, and deal in *name-calling*. The bottom line of a message is the deeper *feelings and needs*. I still remember Rick and Priscilla, since they have become my classic example of this point. I asked Pris to pick a common fight; this time she and Rick were to try to express their feelings and their core needs. They would attempt to go bottom line.

Pris started off, "Rick wants to buy a boat. It's a dumb idea and we can't afford it." I thought, "Oh no, this has been gone over countless, fruitless times" and I stopped Pris right there. I encouraged her to start over, only this time help Rick and me understand what she was feeling and needing. As the story unfolded, Pris was the person in the family responsible for writing the checks for bills. She had been raised in a poor family and poverty scared her. She figured any kind of boat would destroy the balanced budget which she so desperately needed. The purchase of a boat scared her to death.

Rick had grown up in a family where a fishing/ski boat had been the center of many happy family times. He saw himself and Pris drifting apart and thought a boat would help secure his need for a happy and solid family life. As they continued to talk, the boat and surface issues became unimportant as they began dealing with their needs for a balanced budget, a closer relationship, and meeting their individual fears and anxiety. As they cut to the chase, the debating, rehashing, and name-calling stopped. Intimacy thrives on deeper communication—of needs and feelings.

● TIME OUT

1. Take a sheet of paper and list your top five needs in the marriage and try to guess what your mate's top five will be. Exchange papers and discuss.
2. Pick a topic that is emotionally laden for your mate and help him/her describe and explore all the feelings. Help each other grow more skillful in expressing underlying feelings and needs.

---

3. Well-timed. This is such a commonsense factor of an effective message, but still it is often violated. When do you think it would be poor timing, especially for deeper discussion or confrontation? Alcoholics Anonymous uses the acronym H.A.L.T. to help its members be aware when they are vulnerable to altering their mood with a drink. This is a good acronym for poor timing in communication too: *Hungry, Angry, Lonely, Tired.* When your mate gets home after a tough day at work and is starved, that is not the time to resolve a conflict. When you are livid in your belief that you have been deeply wronged, that is not the time to confront in a detached, secure manner. If you are lonely and feeling isolated from your mate, there are greater priorities to attack (like the exclusion and lack of intimacy) than Susy's poor grades. Fatigue can destroy perspective, self-esteem, and diplomatic assertiveness.

The timing of a message is important, but you can also err by waiting for the "perfect" time. It is destructive to *gunnysack* and stuff your feelings, to tiptoe around *avoiding* conflict, to treat your mate as *fragile* and hesitate confronting given behaviors. You have to strike a balance between HALT and nonassertive avoidance or gunnysacking. As their marriage became more and more harassed with busyness, Alex and Jenny struggled with timing. They always seemed hungry, angry, lonely, or tired. They discovered that if problems were neglected for a week, what could have been easily cleared up grew into a major fight. They therefore tried to carve out time for communication and not avoid tensions. The busier they became, the tougher it grew to practice effective timing even though they knew its importance.

● TIME OUT

1. Think of a time in your marriage recently when a message was poorly timed. Is this common? What is creating the poor timing? How could you be more effective?
2. An important message in any marriage that demands good timing is the initiation and refusing of sexual overtures. Discuss the question of timing with your mate. Is there a need for more assertiveness? Do you need to be more tuned into H.A.L.T.? If you refuse, do you negotiate another better time?

---

4. Positive. The best way to understand the importance of keeping messages positive is to explore the destructive nature of negative messages. As they neglected relational problems, Bruce and Nancy got on a more and more negative roll in their messages to each other. A typical conversation would go:

Nancy: "Bruce, you never get home on time any more from work."

Bruce: "You never give me a break these days, do you, Nance? If only you had the time and affirmation for me like you do for our dog, much less the children!"

Nancy (with voice raised): "Don't talk to me about time, when you spend so much time with your mom. You've spent four hours this week with her already."

Bruce: "I give up! I'm going to take a shower."

Positive messages *eliminate words like "never, always"* which carry judgment and are not accurate. *Blaming "you" language* is turned around and the individual takes responsibility with "I" statements. This is also true of *reversing use of the negative "not"* and making a positive statement. "You don't" is changed to "I need you to affirm me more." *Guilt trips, power plays, and hitting below the belt* give way to clean, assertive messages; there is no need for *scorekeeping*. Discourteous techniques like *raising the volume* and *withdrawing* are lovingly refrained from. Bruce and Nancy were indeed on a roll, with their negative messages taking a terrible toll on their communication and marriage. Their negativity also kept their messages from being one-track, bottom-line, and well-timed.

● TIME OUT

1. What negative messages do you lapse into the easiest? Who did you learn them from? Do they sometimes seem effective? Which ones would you really like to change?
2. Take Bruce and Nancy's negative messages and try to clean them up. With your partner, create a scenario with only positive messages coming from Bruce and Nancy.

CREATIVE CONFLICT AND CONFRONTATION

When two unique people with wills of their own marry, they will naturally have differences and conflicts. These differences can separate and distance them, or can be worked through for greater closeness. Conflict is not fun, but it is a necessary part of intimacy. When couples tell me they never fight, I feel like taking their pulse to see if they are alive. Here are important skills for keeping conflict energizing to a relationship and leading to resolution.

1. Practice effective communication skills. All of the communication skills are important for conflict but especially these:

— *Detach* and try to understand your mate, gather information and *dialogue*. If you are out to win or desperately want to change someone, you will never confront and fight effectively.

— Remain *courteous* and take responsibility for your own needs and feelings with *"I language."* Increased volume and blaming attacks go nowhere.

— *Stick to one topic* and head for the deeper level of communication of *needs and feelings*. Creative conflict and confrontation must deal with individual needs and feelings that differ.

2. Become comfortable with conflict. Most people have a fear of conflict and tend to avoid it at all costs. Our fears may originate from scars from angry family arguments, a gentle nature that wants everyone to like us, or poor debate skills. For whatever reasons, we must quit avoiding fights and confrontations if we want intimacy to flourish. We must get comfortable with conflict and practice and practice. It is the only way to learn.

3. Pick your battles. Some things are not worth fighting over. If you have seven points of contention, pick the two most important. Otherwise, in your nitpicking, you will not be heard when you have a crucial difference or point to make. Choose carefully the things you cannot live with and accept—only make a stand on those items.

4. Keep perspective. Arguments and confrontation that get too intense degenerate into ugliness. Take a ten-minute break, hold your breath and count to twenty, try to see your mate's perspective, above all keep your sense of humor. Couples can choose actions or words that trigger laughter which always restores a lighter touch. Don't lose your important points in anger and intensity.

5. Set limits. Know when to stop even if it means agreeing to disagree. Do you really accomplish that much more by

talking half the night than by stopping earlier and agreeing
on a time to reschedule the fight? Anger must be controlled.
Each mate knows when an argument is escalating into the
destructive and should quit right then. If you start spewing
ugliness, there will be no hope of resolution.

6. *Learn to reconcile.* It is amazing what words like, "I'm
sorry," "I really do love you," "You're making some good
points; let me think about them," will accomplish. Somehow
in the midst of conflict, they stick in our throat; but if we can
apologize and affirm our love, they have a soothing and
healing effect. Humility and gentleness go a long way.

7. *Negotiate and seek solutions.* Remember that the purpose
of conflict and confrontation is to resolve differences, not to
win. Couples need to mutually seek tentative compromises
and solutions. This may be to agree to disagree, or put the
issue on hold. It could be a behavioral solution negotiated
around each mate's needs and feelings, a solution both are
willing to try to implement. It is important not to let arguments just drop, but to seek tentative solutions.

● TIME OUT

1. What communication and conflict skills do you violate
   the quickest in the heat of conflict? Is this similar to your
   parents? Where did you learn your conflict skills?
2. Practice a couple of fights with your mate and try to come
   up with effective ways for the two of you to keep perspective and stop escalating fights. Practice apologizing after
   each simulated fight.
3. Brainstorm five possible solutions to your three most
   common arguments.

CHAPTER ELEVEN

Growing Beyond Extramarital Affairs

✠

*T*hou shalt not commit adultery" is probably the best known of the Ten Commandments and yet so many Christian couples get caught in this devastating trap. As we explored the marriage of Norm and Sandi Jennings, we observed what a killer of commitment and intimacy affairs can be. To help you better understand the effects of sexual infidelity, this chapter will explore the five phases of an affair: *inception, prediscovery, discovery, recovery,* and *resolution.* Some affairs never are discovered, but the relationship still has to go through a recovery process. Not every marriage recovers from adultery and reaches a resolution phase.

As we begin, it is important to challenge the myth that adultery is one sin that permanently damages a marriage and can never truly be healed. Most marriages do survive affairs and can grow stronger than they were. Healing is possible even though it is a grueling process, a difficult roller coaster of emotions, with deep anger and grieving. Much courage and patience is required, but a potentially great marriage saved is worth all the effort.

THE INCEPTION PHASE

Adultery begins in a variety of ways. For Norm, it was unchecked curiosity, a deteriorating marriage, and a loss of spiritual integrity. He made a series of poor choices before he ended up in bed with Alison. Bob, Norm's friend, at first fell into affairs because of the thrill of the chase and the ego boost he received. For both Norm and Bob, there was something appealing about the illicitness and the sense of excitement and sexual adventure.

It would be misleading to think that affairs are primarily sexual in their motivation and inception. As with Bob's need for attention and his intimate friendship with Betty, many affairs have nothing to do with surges of hormones, sexual curiosity, or adventure. They sneak up on people and blindside them with a need for a listening ear, emotional closeness, or escape. They may inadvertently fall in love or try to meet their nonsexual needs (affirmation, being special) sexually.

Jan and Bill had a solid marriage. Their sex life was good and they had fun sharing a variety of recreational and spiritual activities together. Jan was surprised when she admitted to herself she had developed a strong attraction and some sexual feelings and fantasies for Winston, the church youth leader whom she helped with the teens. She thought about him quite often. They had a longstanding and warm friendship in which they discussed the intimate details of their lives. He made her feel special. She was even more startled when they both acted on their attraction and sexualized the friendship impulsively after a youth meeting at his place.

A great deal of guilt ensued, since she truly loved Bill; somehow her relationship with both her husband and Winston changed. With hindsight, Jan discovered that what she really needed from Winston was a caring intimacy and a validation of her femininity. But as happens so often in a tragic way when nonsexual needs evolve into sexual intimacy, she completely destroyed the possibility of Winston's further friendship and support. Something was permanently altered when she crossed the sexual line.

Jan discovered too late the myth that claims affairs can be relatively harmless. She and many others rationalize when contemplating adultery or beginning an affair, "This need not affect my personal network of mate, children, friends, the work place, or ministry. Should it be discovered—but it probably won't be—things will quickly return to the way they were." More often in an affair, one's nest has been dirtied, and there is irreparable damage to certain friendships and relationships.

I am sure you could come up with examples of long-term affairs or short-term flings where the marriage did not seem to be affected. I would suggest that at some level commitment was broken and honesty, trust, and respect violated. A deeper level of intimacy in both relationships was sacrificed. With hindsight, Jan realized she had ignored many of the warnings that could have helped her prevent the affair.

– Do not keep secrets and allow sexual feelings and fantasies to go unaddressed.

– Do not permit an intimate friendship with the opposite sex to grow without tight boundaries (e.g., my mate is included, any sexual attraction will end the friendship, no secret letters or phone calls).

– Do not share intimate details of your marriage, mate, and self with an opposite sex friend.

– Do not spend unaccounted for time together.

Bill noticed Winston was treating him differently and that the relationship between Jan and Winston had altered somehow. The whole story finally came out because Jan needed the healing and the chance to rebuild the honesty, trust, and closeness she valued with Bill. She deeply grieved that her actions had destroyed her friendship with Winston.

She and Bill tried to repair the damage and go on with business as usual, but it did not work. Any contact with Winston triggered mistrust in Bill and Jan did not like the feelings for Winston that were so quickly rekindled. Finally she and Bill mutually decided to find another church home and avoid all contact in order to promote healing in their marriage. Jan felt this was a step she had to take as she tried to repair what she had destroyed. She felt deep remorse and sadness for Bill, the innocent victim who got caught in the fallout from her poor choices.

Extramarital affairs indeed have many causes and can happen in relatively good marriages. Sometimes with hindsight a couple will discover marital flaws they were not aware of that actually did make them vulnerable to an affair. Adultery can result from sexual curiosity, need for romance, poor sex life with one's mate, or falling in love and evolving into sexual intimacy. Affairs can also indicate nonsexual needs for affirmation and love, to be listened to and gently held. Some people use affairs to get revenge, or to try to end a marriage, or they pursue them out of their own craziness.

This personal craziness can take many forms, with the sexual affair being a *symptom* of deeper problems that need to be addressed. If a person is in the middle of a midlife crisis, an affair may seem a way to deal with the need for validation and the desire to feel young and sexy again. A husband may act out and relive his family background—his dad set a great example of keeping intimacy at a distance by a series of affairs. A woman sexually abused as a child may feel that the only way to get male validation is to be seductive; she repeatedly is revictimized by the men in her life.

Sexual addicts may use sex like any other drug to alter their moods; they may have affairs, not because they are attracted to someone, but because they are bored or depressed or feeling guilty and see this as a way to change those feelings. Sexual adultery (or pornography or voyeurism or masturbation) is simply a means to get excitement, counter guilt, or feel less depressed and desperate. If affairs are a symptom of deeper personal issues, then those problems must be dealt with as a part of the therapeutic process.

● TIME OUT_____

1. What type of an extramarital affair would you be most vulnerable to? Sometimes our strengths (sensitivity, outgoingness) are the chinks in our armor which Satan attacks. Analyze the last time you contemplated an affair and what needs it would have met. What relational deficits and what individual craziness could make you susceptible? Are you violating any of the warning flags right now?
2. Discuss with your mate the following myths:
    ● Affairs happen only in bad marriages.
    ● Both mates always contribute to an affair.
    ● There are safe affairs where one's nest is not dirtied.
    ● Adultery is one sin that is almost impossible to heal.
    ● An affair could never happen to us.

THE PREDISCOVERY PHASE

Some affairs are so short-lived they never go through the prediscovery phase. That is not to say a one-night stand is not destructive or may not precipitate a discovery and recovery phase. This stage is when the adulterous relationship comes into full bloom with guilt, excitement, much phone time, dishonesty, and a lot of craziness. The cheater has to hone up on dishonesty skills as he or she attempts to balance two worlds and successfully weave a web of deceit. This is a nerve-racking process with the adventure of the chase, excitement of the illicit, guilt of hurting the marriage, warmth of added intimacy, and the confusion over what is being done to one's mate and commitment. It is quite a feat to compartmentalize and juggle two relationships, keeping them separate and appeased. Time becomes an important commodity.

The one cheated on is also thrown into confusion and anger, often without any knowledge of what is really going on. Sandi knew Norm wasn't himself, but she could not quite put a finger on it. She thought he took a little extra care with his appearance and knew he had actually bought himself some new cologne. He spent more time away, and yet at other times he was almost solicitous. She was a little startled, though appreciative, when flowers came for no particular reason. Norm never sent flowers except for Valentine's Day and special anniversaries. He seemed more critical at times and wanted her to buy a red outfit, although they both knew she looked terrible in red. One night her sexiest nightgown did not have its usual effect, though they did end up finally making love.

Sandi saw the relationship was out of whack, but she wasn't sure why. She and Norm could not get in sync, and they did not play or joke or hug as much. She thought maybe it was his heavier job demands; he seemed a little young for a midlife crisis. Maybe she was losing her appeal. This *could* be all her fault, though that didn't fit very well either. Perhaps both needed to go on a Marriage Encounter weekend or take a vacation. Their marriage might just be going stale; yet, everything sure had a crazy feel to it.

The person involved in the affair is often oblivious to the changes taking place: the different behavior patterns, the negative thinking regarding the mate, the rationalizing and crazy thought patterns. Norm later admitted he was not aware of how blatant his behaviors became as he pursued Alison and Kim. He knew Sandi was becoming less and less attractive to him, but he thought it was more her doing than his. He became convinced in his convoluted thinking that an affair was probably the only way to rescue the marriage. Commitment, right and wrong, lust, and caring all became blurred to him; Sandi lived in perpetual confusion.

The prediscovery stage goes on until the affair ends or is discovered. The guilt sometimes decreases as the marriage becomes secondary and the adulterous behaviors get more careless. The marriage companionship steadily deteriorates as negative feelings build for both mates. Betrayal creates anger and avoidance. Anger brings resentment and increased fighting. Happiness and intimacy are replaced by suspicion, irritableness, blame, and a sense of hopelessness.

Extramarital affairs often end before discovery, for a variety of reasons. The affair may have been a brief fling out of curiosity or a need for appreciation or nurture. One or both parties in the adultery may grow weary of the confusion or be fearful of losing their marriage or job, and end it. The adulterer's values may kick in; or he or she may discover a desire for their mate and renew efforts to make marriage work. Sometimes the one being cheated on will force a confrontation and bring about change, without the affair being discovered.

Whether or not the affair is discovered, there are repercussions from the betrayal that must be resolved. Even if undiscovered, the adulterer will need to go through some of the healing steps of the discovery, recovery, and resolution phases. Issues like, "Why did it happen? How do I repair commitment? What is appropriate confession and forgiveness?" will have to be addressed.

An issue most people struggle with is the advisability of confessing undiscovered affairs, both past and present. Confession is vital in restoring honesty, rebuilding trust, and feeling the unconditional accepting warmth of intimacy. It acknowledges that a given behavior was destructive (sinful) and brings it to the light of day so the power of secrecy and guilt can be broken. It helps the guilty one feel accepted and forgiven, in spite of what he or she has done. As James 5:16 encourages us, "Confess your sins to each other and pray for each other so that you may be healed." An ongoing or very recent affair usually demands confession to one's mate as well as to God and His representative, for healing to begin to take place.

Jan resisted at first, but found she would have to tell Bill all that had happened with Winston for there to be healing. There was no way for her to reclaim honesty and rebuild trust without a complete and fearless inventory of all that had happened. The subsequent anger and confusion fogged their perspective so much that Jan and Bill realized they would need a helping professional to guide them through the anger and betrayal and guilt. This helped the confession and forgiving to produce the healing they desired.

The appropriateness of confessing past affairs is more difficult to determine. Two different examples will illustrate this. Jimmy confessed to me he had had a one-nighter four years ago while on the road as a salesman. He still experienced guilt and wondered if he should tell Margie. As we sorted it through, it seemed he had already worked through forgiveness; to unload on Margie would be sharing the guilt more than taking a step toward healing. He decided not to tell her, and that I was the more appropriate confessor. We made sure there was no residual dishonesty or broken intimacy.

Jodi had had three extramarital affairs over the twelve years of her marriage, the last one happening two years ago. She came into counseling because she was contemplating adultery once again and wanted to break the destructive pattern. We decided she would have to bring her husband, Ed, into it, even though the adultery was long over. She wished to enlist him in her forgiveness and change process, and saw confessing all as a necessary part of that. It was a painful but encouraging time of discovery and growth for both of them.

Sometimes confession is best done to God and one of His representatives who can help you work through guilt and dishonesty, and then experience forgiveness. But often the mate has to be involved to restore honesty and reestablish commitment and intimacy.

● TIME OUT _____

1. Do you think an affair is less destructive if it is never discovered? Why is confession important? When and how would you confess?
2. What are some of the telltale signs an affair is going on? How would you confront your mate or a friend? Why do you think the prediscovery phase has such a devastating effect on the marriage?

_____

THE DISCOVERY PHASE

A profusion of feelings, issues, and reactions must be worked through during this third phase of discovery. The manner in which the affair is discovered, whether accidental, intentional, or somewhere in-between, doesn't seem to matter. It is a great shock, whether it is confessed, or discovered via taped phone conversations, a private detective, or a growing collection of evidence and a confrontation. It throws both mates into a new stage of the marriage with pain, guilt, betrayal, and deep loss. Choices have to be made and a *grieving process* is entered.

Elizabeth Kubler-Ross and others have demonstrated there are various stages and feelings people go through when they are grieving a loss. Grieving is a vital part of the discovery and recovery phases because *multiple losses* have been incurred by both marital partners in an affair: respect, the marriage as it was, self-esteem, commitment, dreams and expectations, and trust. The first reaction in grieving is usually shock and denial that this could really be happening. Later stages and reactions in the grieving process include anger in many manifestations, intense and wildly fluctuating emotions and tears, depression, bargaining and interrogation, confrontation and many flashbacks. All of the stages have to be worked through before healing can occur and the adultery be resolved.

When Bob decided he had to tell his wife, Jill, about his affairs, he expected her to react with instant anger or tears and to already suspect what was going on. Instead, Jill sat there numbly as if it couldn't quite sink in and did not make sense. She had not suspected and couldn't believe this was happening to them and their marriage. Bob continued to talk and told her how he had met Betty at school and quite unintentionally fallen in love with her, and that he was not sure of the marriage anymore.

Bob felt such relief to get everything out in the open but was not prepared for Jill's reaction in the coming days: deep pain like a black cloud, intense hostility with hate in her eyes, and an endless interrogation. She wanted to know: When did he and Betty get together? Where and how many times? Who else knew? What about other affairs? Could she ever trust him? etc. etc. Bob grew weary, but out of a sense of guilt and penitence tried to help with her anger and questions as they both became exhausted.

Bob struggled deeply with grief and loss too, for though he had chosen to work at his marriage, he had grown to truly love Betty and missed their conversations as much as the sex. They had grown into a very intimate and comfortable companionship. The sex was special too and so much better than what he and Jill experienced. Somehow Betty made him feel happy and he missed that. He felt compassion for Jill, but needed someone to lean on as he grieved the loss of the affair. What a terrible roller coaster of hurt, desires, shame, and grief.

After the discovery of adultery most couples go through as many turbulent feelings as Bob and Jill experienced. They have to slowly progress beyond the shock and denial into the following grief work of anger, tears, depression, interrogation, and working through to acceptance and healing. Bob felt definite relief to have the secrets disclosed, but was confused as he tried to follow through on choices, fearing he would lose both Betty and Jill. He struggled with wanting to keep Betty on hold, while he explored whether the marriage could be rebuilt. Jill hung in there but stated assertively that he would have to make a choice. Her self-respect would not allow her to live in limbo. Bob slowly realized that to maintain any contact with Betty was not fair to either woman and would sabotage the healing process. The discovery phase began for him a tough and willful journey of grieving as he let go of thoughts, feelings, and contact with Betty.

The discovery phase, Bob learned, was not just the discovery, uncovering, of the extramarital affair. He and Jill underwent an intensive exploration and discovery of what was going on in their lives and in the marriage. Why did Betty make him happier? What changes did he and Jill need to make? This process would continue into the following stage but was very intense the first few weeks. They kicked around everything from sexual inhibitions to ego-stroking, from lack of commitment and quality time to their family backgrounds. All the pieces of the puzzle did not fall into place, but they did find some plausible answers — from Bob's fear of responsibility to Jill's inability to relax.

Jill grew increasingly angry as she wallowed through her devastating loss, feeling deeply betrayed. She wondered how she could have been so stupid and gullible. She should have caught on to what was going on and not let it go on so long. Rationally she knew, and her counselor reminded her, that an affair was foreign to her trust and image of Bob. She would have to forgive herself for being human and unaware. In this discovery phase Sandi too felt very duped by both Norm and Alison. How could they have played her for such a sucker? She was better able to get beyond the egg on her face when she shifted the responsibility for the adultery to where it belonged: Norm and Alison. She also learned to cut herself some slack and, like Jill, admit she was human.

Bill felt naive and foolish and remained angry over Jan's adultery. He also felt terrible because something he thought was unique and special to their relationship had been shared with another. Bill would have nightmares of Winston and Jan together sexually and got so he did not want to make love with Jan at all. He would wonder if she was thinking about him or Winston during sex. It wasn't just the sex; he was troubled by the emotional betrayal and that Winston had replaced him in their companionship. He wondered if the relationship would ever be the same again.

● TIME OUT _____

1. In losses in your life, which is the most difficult stage of the grieving process for you to work through? Shock and denial? Anger, tears, and depression? Sorting and interrogation? Acceptance and healing?

2. What part of an affair do you think is the worst betrayal? Sexual? Duping one's mate? Sharing love and companionship?

3. What parts of a support network will a couple need to put in place, in addition to a committed mate, in order to grow through the discovery and healing of an affair?

THE RECOVERY PHASE

Bill was able to work through his feelings with the help of some counseling. The marriage slowly began recovering from the infidelity. He realized that the most serious damage and threat to their marriage and commitment was the emotional and relational betrayal, not the physical. He sorted through how he sometimes viewed Jan as property which had become damaged goods, rather than as a hurting person who wanted to reestablish an intimate relationship. The ultimate betrayal was not the physical act of sexual intercourse but rather the breaking of commitment, the dishonesty, and the damaged trust.

Bill came to grips with the fact that his marriage had much more glue and uniqueness than just sexual faithfulness. Many couples drift so far apart that the only bond between them is that they do not have sex with anyone else. When this bond is broken, the marriage is in jeopardy. Bill and Jan enjoyed so much love and many common interests. This helped carry them through as they healed the broken bond of fidelity.

In the recovery as well as the discovery stage, the 1,001 questions continue, waking up the adulterer in the middle of the night or firing a barrage the minute he or she gets home from work. A wrong number, a new sexual technique, twenty extra minutes getting home at night and the angry, attacking questions begin all over again. It seems like trust will never be rebuilt.

Especially in the discovery stage, but also in the recovery, I will tell people that adultery is like a funeral and you need to view the body. Mates need a thoroughly honest confession to validate a real loss has taken place and to slowly grieve and reclaim the marriage. Couples need to explore what went wrong to prevent repeat occurrences. But the questioning can become very counterproductive, as the cheated on moves from viewing the body into a crazy, obsessive, repetitive autopsy.

I have wondered why all the questions and painful drilling take place. I think the mate who was cheated on is trying:

– to break through shock and denial and ventilate some anger as the grieving process is worked through,

– to prevent with enough questions and knowledge another affair from happening,

– to completely reclaim the mate by destroying all secrets and having everything in the relationship once again mutually shared,

– to exact some penance and perhaps vengeance as the partner squirms.

In the interrogation, the most healthy questions are *process-oriented* – what is missing in our relationship? How did the love grow for someone else? What help do we need? *Detail* questions – when, where, how many times, what positions – create vivid nightmares. The mate who was cheated on must resist fantasies and allowing the imagination to run wild.

It is not unusual to encounter a need for vengeance or restitution. One of my clients told his wife that since she had had an affair, he was going to sleep with five different women or with one woman five times. I am not sure why the number five stuck in his mind. Others will assign their mate some onerous task, "You can unload the dishwasher for the rest of our marriage." Actually, making amends or restitution is a scriptural idea. After his conversion, Zaccheus stated he would pay back four times the amount to anyone he had cheated as a tax collector and Christ saw true penance and repentance in this act (Luke 19:8). Ezekiel 33:14-16 encourages that if a person "turns away from his sin and does what is just and right . . . returns what he has stolen, follows the decrees that give life, and does no evil, he will surely live."

An adulterer has stolen intimacy and commitment from his or her partner. Restitution in kind seems appropriate, not only to heal what has been damaged but also to help the person grow through penitence and then reestablish trust. This does not mean vengeance or destructive restitution like five affairs, but rather that time, money, and energy be invested in rebuilding the marital intimacy that has been so damaged by the adultery.

Usually the one involved in the affair is ready to move on long before the wounded partner and grows weary in the recovery process. The initial choice of forgiveness on both partners' part may be done quickly, but the process of forgiving, letting go, and rebuilding respect and trust takes time. One man stated in a therapy session, "She has forgiven me; I don't know why she can't forget and trust me again." This was said after two weeks had elapsed since the discovery of his third affair. I quickly replied, "I wouldn't trust you as far as I could throw you right now. You don't have much of a track record."

The recovery stage is obviously different for various couples depending on the condition of their marriage before the adultery, their individual issues and craziness, and the depth of the affair. As time went on, Bob realized how much he loved Jill and how he really wanted to honor God's will and rebuild the marriage. But he learned that it would not be an easy process. Fortunately Jill understood this and on her good days remained objective, as they both put their boots on and waded into the mess of rebuilding their relationship. Bob did not begin an endless series of good-byes with Betty, but tried to quit cold turkey. Except for two relapses — one phone call and one brief visit which he quickly confessed — the healing slowly took place.

He tried to see the two relationships, Jill and Betty, as apples and oranges that should not be compared. He was into apples now and he wanted to believe his counselor's advice that the quality of intimacy he built with Jill would exceed what he had with Betty, different but better. On tough days when Betty would pop into his thoughts, he would take the card out of his wallet on which he had written a list of positive things about Jill and the marriage on one side, and all the negative things about Betty and the affair on the other side. He would go over these to jog his mind back into perspective. Bob worked hard on displacement, or maybe it could be called replacement. He concentrated on crowding out the thoughts of oranges (Betty) with thoughts of apples (Jill and God's will for his life). He knew that it would not work to leave a vacuum in his life (Matthew 12:43-45); he truly wanted Jill to take the place of Betty.

The process was more difficult than he thought it would be, requiring constant work and willpower. The biggest hurdle was truly committing to make the marriage work and humbly opening himself up to value apples and Jill. As he looked back later, Bob realized it was actually a series of choices. For a long time, in his skepticism and attachment to Betty, he truly did not let Jill back into his heart and desires. He thought he had made a choice, but it was indeed half-hearted at first.

Jill struggled through her own grieving and letting go during this recovery process. She had to work through a cloud of anger, betrayal, self-pity, and intense jealousy. At work, or while they were making love or out together, something would trigger the affair in her mind and she would flare up. It didn't help that in his initial confession, Bob had been so sketchy that as new facts emerged, she doubted his truthfulness. Jill got better at identifying the triggers and talking through them. She did not like the crazy, nagging, angry person she had become. She tried to follow her therapist's suggestions and deal with some of these flashbacks in counseling or while talking to her best friend who knew about the affair. She knew Bob needed the chance to heal and rebuild trust. Sometimes she was able to dump it on her friend or therapist, but other times she would jump Bob all over again with accusations and interrogation. It was a confusing, painful time for both.

They wondered early in recovery if there would ever be an end or a resolution—forgiveness and healing was such a slow process. With patience and renewed commitment, both worked at restoring stability and loving companionship to their marriage. The awkward job of rebuilding sexuality, supporting relationships, and a mutual connectedness took time. Fortunately their intimacy had not been completely destroyed and Betty was outside their main network of friends. Their nest was not badly soiled.

One difficult area was Jill's parents. She had used them as confidants and for support after the discovery of the affair, when the marriage was up in the air. Jill painfully discovered that using parents this way could backfire badly. Her folks had a difficult time taking Bob back into the family and working through their own anger and forgiveness.

Marriages in which the adultery is never discovered may still go through a recovery and resolution phase. This can include marriage counseling or perhaps a renewed effort to reestablish intimacy with more time together and greater sexual frequency. Grieving over the losses may also occur. The predicament is doing this important work somewhat blindly — at least one partner is in the dark. The danger is that the work will be done halfway or not at all, leaving the offender very vulnerable to another affair. The honesty, trust, and commitment may never truly be healed and the needs that motivated the affair never addressed.

If you have an undiscovered affair, please make sure it has truly been dealt with. It would be worth exploring it with a marriage counselor to see if any residual causes are still lurking, so that the factors which contributed to your cheating won't come back to haunt you.

Not everyone in the recovery stage chooses to stay married. Sometimes the couple sees themselves as having drifted too far apart and the affair as the final straw. Trust may be irreparably shattered as the couple tries to pick up the pieces but cannot. The adultery may have been a symptom of deeper individual craziness or relational problems which never get resolved. After evaluating the marriage, the one in the affair may decide to get a divorce and marry the person with whom they had the affair. History has shown this to be dangerous. Affairs are *very idealistic* and are not the best perspective from which to choose a life partner.

As a therapist I sometimes get impatient with widows who idealize their dead mates; but I feel even more exasperated with people in extramarital affairs. They will say, "I'm so happy." "Sex has never been this good." "He is so understanding and actually listens to me." "We picked each other out of a crowd — it seems preordained." I will say, "What do you expect? You're disgusted with your own mate and feeling disconnected, sensual, and bored. You see your lover at a planned time when you are rested, well-groomed, and at your best. Are you surprised it feels good? I ask what their marriage and sex life would be like if they devoted the same kind of time and attention to it.

Adultery does not have to be the final nail in the coffin. The damage of an extramarital affair and the difficulty in healing seem to depend on a variety of factors:

– the length and intensity of the affair, especially feelings of love and friendship,

– the state of the marriage before, during, and after the affair,

– the level of individual craziness and the amount of environmental pressures (financial, illness) in addition to the affair,

– the depth of dishonesty, broken commitment, disrespect, and the breakdown of intimacy,

– the willingness to make changes.

Some couples have a honeymoon period during the recovery phase. This is understandable and on the positive side; it can help to heal wounds. On the negative side, it can sweep under the rug issues which will later come back to haunt the marriage. The one involved in the affair is so relieved to be beyond the secrecy and guilt, and to be reconnected to the mate. The one cheated on, after dealing with anger and betrayal, is excited not to have lost a mate. After their marriage had such a close call, both have their adrenaline flowing and deeply appreciate that the disaster was averted. Sex has been forced out in the open and romantic awareness increased, with warm feelings and libido running high.

Howard and Dawn were three weeks past the discovery of his affair and offer a good example of the honeymoon phenomenon. They were deeply committed to each other again and feeling very much in love, almost like giddy teenagers. Dawn had forgiven him for the adultery, which wasn't that difficult because she herself had had a close call only the month before out of boredom and frustration. Suddenly Howard's job that had been so time-consuming seemed less important and he was coming home earlier. Dawn was doing better at minimizing the constant demands of the children. They made love like they did the first year of their marriage and just couldn't seem to get enough of each other. They would talk until two in the morning even though Howard wasn't a night person. They looked forward to being together and exchanged special glances. The value and intimacy of their marriage seemed firmly reestablished.

● TIME OUT_____

1. How would you suggest an individual and a couple take an undiscovered affair through the healing recovery process? What are the pitfalls in working through an undisclosed secret? How could they be overcome?
2. In what creative ways could an adulterer compensate and give a mate restitution? How would this help?
3. What do you feel are the most important factors that contribute to a marriage surviving an affair and finally healing?

THE RESOLUTION PHASE

The couples working on recovery slowly reestablished the equilibrium and intimacy in their relationships. Now came a very crucial time in each of their marriages — the final resolution phase of an affair as the healing process would merge back into the humdrum of routine existence. As the grief and causes of the adultery are worked through, the marriage is either put back together stronger and continues to grow, or settles back into the same ruts and craziness and is prone to future affairs.

Bob and Jill continued to go to marriage counseling. As the fog of the adultery settled down, they began to objectively make changes in their relationship and themselves to affair-proof their marriage. They enrolled in a joint Bible study and Bob assumed the leadership for making their faith more of a shared experience. They created a better support network and made themselves accountable to other Christians. They each built even closer same-sex friendships and determined not to keep secrets. Norm and Bob became even more intimate as Norm got his life back on track. They now meet weekly for fellowship and self-disclosing confession.

Both Bob and Jill thought through and discussed their boundaries — for appropriate or inappropriate behavior. Bob

determined never to meet with another woman (business lunch, church planning) without telling Jill first. Jill wanted to set better limits in their sexual joking, especially with one couple who were intimate friends. They also set in place some red flags that they would immediately take action on when they popped up:
- any keeping of secrets,
- sexual infrequency in their marriage,
- avoiding fellowship and accountability,
- gunnysacking of anger,
- any continued thinking or fantasizing about a member of the opposite sex,
- feeling distanced from God.

The emotional and spiritual growth came tough as they continually resisted sliding back into old patterns and ruts. The scars of the affairs still haunted them occasionally; they did not try to avoid or ignore them, but talked about them. They were encouraged to see the progress and God was blessing as He had promised. They claimed the promise of 2 Chronicles 7:14: "If My people, who are called by My name, will humble themselves and pray and seek My face and turn from their wicked ways, then will I hear from heaven and will forgive their sin and will heal."

Howard and Dawn enjoyed the honeymoon period and felt depressed as the relationship bogged down once again with the extreme time demands of his work and the taxing burden of two children. They tried to keep each other a priority and communicated better. Dawn's temper remained an issue as well as Howard's tendency to withdraw from conflict and passively express his anger through logic and sarcasm. Howard was surprised when only a year and a half after the affair he was seriously tempted to engage in another. Unfortunately, adultery and its causes are not easily swept under the rug. There are many Howards and Dawns in this world who end up in the same dilemma until they finally make necessary changes.

● TIME OUT

1. Make a list of all the causes (individual, marital, sexual, nonsexual) of affairs you can think of—are any of these

present in your marriage? Please, please make needed changes.
2. What are the sexual and relationship boundaries in your marriage? What is permissible behavior for your mate? With a group? With a member of the opposite sex?
3. With your mate discuss and write down the red warning flags each will recognize, when you or the marriage is becoming affair-prone. Remember Norm, Jan, and others made a whole series of poor choices and ignored all the flags.

Extramarital affairs in all their phases are complex and at times unique to a given couple. Overall though, there is a lot of commonality, and any affair is a destructive dragon. If you have not done the exercises, please go back and sort through your own vulnerabilities and set up some red warning flags. This chapter could spare your marriage much grief and lost companionship. No one is invulnerable to adultery; my desire is that you do not get blindsided.

For Further Reading

Les Carter, *The Prodigal Spouse: How to Survive Infidelity.* Nashville: Thomas Nelson Publishers, 1990.

Donald M. Joy, *Rebounding: Preventing and Restoring Damaged Relationships.* Dallas: Word Publishing, 1986.

Richard Exley, *Perils of Power: Immorality in the Ministry.* Tulsa: Honor Books/Harrison House, Inc., 1988.

Frank Pittman, *Private Lies: Infidelity and the Betrayal of Intimacy.* New York: W.W. Norton & Company, 1989.

CHAPTER TWELVE

Putting Sex Back into Your Marriage

✠

A recent television show featured a character who was supposedly married simultaneously to thirteen different women. He was able to accomplish this feat and keep them all satisfied because he was the possessor of a remarkable sexual technique: the Venus Butterfly. This show stirred up a furor of public interest. Everyone wanted to know whether this technique was fact or fiction and how they could learn it. I had clients ask me about it and I assured them it was a myth; so many people want a magical aphrodisiac that will instantly revive a faltering sex life. Couples who fall prey to one or more of the marriage dragons are especially alarmed at the damage that has been done to the sexual aspect of their intimacy.

Like most of life, sexual healing and enrichment are areas where the rewards are equal to the energy invested. There are no easy answers.

This chapter explores three crucial areas for protecting and rejuvenating your lovemaking if you are willing to work, or perhaps I should say, play at it.

— Six common but deadly sabotages of a couple's love life that need to be understood and avoided.

— Five important character traits that every successful lover should develop and nurture.

— Seven enjoyable ways to revive passion and playfulness in your sex life.

SIX SABOTAGES OF
POSITIVE SEXUALITY

It is fascinating that a couple's sex life is often a microcosm, a picture window, a barometer of their whole relationship. Infrequent lovemaking is often indicative of a marriage that is harassed to death by busyness. A couple who cannot comfortably initiate or refuse sex, without getting hurt feelings and pouting, usually experiences poor communication in general. The individual who has difficulty relaxing and letting go of control, as they revel in their sexual feelings, probably struggles with playfulness and enjoying pleasure in other areas of life.

Conversely, a couple with a great love life often has a comfortable, happy companionship; the person who can assertively express sexual needs can usually communicate other personal desires. If the following sexual sabotages are present in your marriage, you may want to examine whether these are skill and attitude deficiencies that impact other areas of your relationship as well as the sexual.

1. Spectatoring. This is a common sabotage where an individual or the couple is up on the bedpost watching what is happening, rather than truly participating in the lovemaking process. Intense, performance-oriented people have trouble fully enjoying the present moment. The husband may be spectatoring as he ponders whether he is a great lover and is satisfying his wife. The wife may be on the bedpost saying, "It's time I climaxed; I'm sure he is getting tired." Performance anxiety and spectatoring seem to always have an opposite negative effect. The man who is worried about impotence, and is on the bedpost watching to see if he can get an erection tonight, never does. The woman worried about achieving an orgasm, and observing from the bedpost, completely sabotages her efforts.

Anna and Scott had been trying together for six months to help her achieve an orgasm and receive the greater sexual enjoyment she desired. After I encouraged them to play at it, Anna started experiencing feelings and focusing in on sensations in ways she had not been able to in the past. Scott was excited and pleased as things changed and he became a loving agent of that change.

But now they were discouraged and at an impasse. Anna had become impatient because she was right on the verge of a climax but could not quite go over the edge, so she got Scott to work harder. He put his best effort into it and became frustrated with himself and Anna. He began to doubt his ability as a lover. All of a sudden both of them were up on the bedpost with tremendous anxiety and frustration. Everything remained at an impasse until they quit spectatoring and reinvolved themselves in the playful process.

The goal of positive lovemaking is a playful, exciting, and tender *connecting*. The sexual verb is *relate*, not score, worry, try harder, or climax. Sex cannot have a job deadline like a critical house repair. A couple needs to resist performance anxiety and create a conducive romantic ambiance as they enjoy the mutual sharing of feelings. Anna achieved an orgasm not long after she and Scott got centered back on playful, exciting connecting and forgot the goal of orgasm.

2. *Imbalance.* I have started calling foreplay *loveplay,* because I dislike the idea that making love is simply a focus on intercourse and orgasm. Couples sabotage and get into terrible ruts by neglecting to create and enjoy a broad range of sexual activity. They make the production of at least one orgasm each the goal of lovemaking. There are five senses; touch is only one of them. This was a major pitfall of Alex and Jenny as they got too busy.

They just did not have the time and energy anymore to remain sensual, relaxed, and varied. They used to include the senses of hearing and smell as they lit scented candles and played soft music. Alex got excited by Jenny's sexy nighties and both took the time for extra touches they knew the other enjoyed. They made the time for playing an hour or more in single lovemaking sessions and were excited about how creative and energized they became with this intimate connecting.

Many couples have quit utilizing the repertoire they once had. Alex and Jenny began enriching their love life by brainstorming and recapturing some of the best of the past. Jenny was upset because they had lost the tender nonsexual hugs and caresses that had led to such great sex. Alex missed the lingerie and playfulness. Together they recaptured the excitement that comes from variety and keeping a balance of sensuality, feelings, and a whole repertoire of activities. They found that when they played the same, they stayed the same—in a rut!

3. Adultery. "Drink water from your own cistern, running water from your own well. . . . May your fountain be blessed, and may you rejoice in the wife of your youth. . . . May her breasts satisfy you always, may you ever be captivated by her love" (Proverbs 5:15-19). The biblical prohibition is not the only reason I refrain from committing adultery. I stay away from affairs because I think a wise, loving Creator has given me a blueprint: monogamy creates the greatest sex in the world. A loving, committed relationship provides the context for developing a level of sexual satisfaction that cannot be matched elsewhere. You know each other's body and pleasure areas; you are comfortable and relaxed and can laugh at silly mistakes; you are in it for the long haul and not just a buzz. Illicit sex is exciting, but the rush wears off.

Even in an affair where there is love and commitment, the dishonesty is crippling. The toxic nature of adultery was explored in chapter 11, but because of its destructive prevalency, I felt compelled to once again mention extramarital affairs as a noxious sabotage of ultimate sexual enjoyment.

4. Lack of structure and priority. Many couples have said to me, "I refuse to structure time for sexual activity; that would completely destroy its fun and spontaneity," to which I reply, "As busy as you are, if you don't plan sex into your life, you will never make love!" One of my supervisors in my sex therapy training, Dr. Domeena Renshaw, said she was always amazed by couples. Here was an activity both would heartily agree was fun, relaxing, and important to them, but they placed it around number twenty-five on their list of priorities and then wrote it in in pencil in case they had to move it lower.

There are few couples whose love life has not been seriously sabotaged by lack of structure and priority. It may be because they start making love at 11 P.M., when one or both of them are physically and emotionally spent. They may try to get all the chores done first or not plan carefully enough around the children. They may make love only when the mood and circumstances are perfect—averaging about once every two months. I am continually startled by the number of loving Christian couples who enjoy sex, but haven't had relations in two to six months. When they do make love, they often wonder why they don't do it more often.

Trip and Heather are a typical couple who had come to see me concerning a problem with Heather's mom. During the intake interview, when I routinely asked about their sex life, they stated they had not made love in two months. As I explored I found that they both enjoyed sex, and were surprised it actually had been two months. Trip was more of a night person and so they went to bed at separate times. The children interfered on weekends. Both enjoyed very active lives and each was out late twice a week. I went into my standard lecture on prioritizing and structuring. We made a few quick adjustments—go to bed at the same time, train the children to respect their locked door and privacy—and they agreed to schedule in lovemaking twice a week.

I tell couples they have to prioritize as they *structure spontaneous sex* back into their marriage. They can plan in sexual activity and also allow for spontaneity. They can easily do it differently every Tuesday night for years as they vary activity, ambiance, place, timing, and technique. I do not think there is a norm for frequency, but most enjoyable bonding activities would be great to include once or twice a week. Sometimes it is a great warning flag for a couple to notice if frequency has dropped under once a week, as they examine their priorities and try to structure.

5. *Wet blankets.* Many circumstances of life as well as ignorance, can have an extremely dampening effect on a couple's sex life. Jordan and Dee weren't sure of all that was wrong in their sex life, but knew it sure was not hitting on all eight cylinders. They could identify several factors. Because Dee had grown up in a very restrictive Christian environment where sex was never talked about, she came to suspect and squelch all sexual feelings. She had also experienced an attempted date rape in her first year of college that had been very traumatizing. Jordan enjoyed sex but was insecure about his skills as a lover. He thought it unfair that society expected

men to know everything about sex, since the major fount of sexual knowledge was the men's locker room.

As we talked further, Dee shared that she had a difficult time relaxing and enjoying sexual feelings. The more they fought about sex and Jordan made demands, the more she shut down. Dee was not comfortable with her body image and thought her breasts were too small. I remember a female colleague of mine who got so upset at the poor body image most women have, she angrily stated, "Why do women's breasts come in only two sizes: too big and too small?"

Dee wished Jordan could empathize more with her sexual needs and feelings. He was more visual and genitally oriented, but she enjoyed tenderness and nonsexual touching and nurturing. I discovered that Dee and Jordan had most of the wet blankets that can sabotage a sex life: *ignorance, traumas,* societal and religious *prohibitions, poor body image,* and *conflict.*

These sexual inhibitors respond well to change strategies. Dee worked through the trauma of her date rape and improved her body image. Jordan learned to be more romantic in his sexual advances. Both grew more comfortable after some reading on sexual response and technique. They were excited as the sexual dimension of their marriage finally began to blossom.

6. *Control and selflessness.* These are not bad traits, but in unhealthy doses they can sabotage sexual fulfillment. Jenny had a strong need to nurture others and be in control of her life. Alex wished she could relax and enjoy her own feelings. She still remembers the night there was a tremendous breakthrough. All day Saturday Jenny had felt especially loved and close to Alex. She actually initiated sexual overtures that night at 1 A.M. after a night on the town. Somehow in her warm connectedness and sleepy lack of inhibition she became more and more involved as she let herself go. She remembers in the middle of lovemaking noticing how turned on Alex had become and what power she had to excite her husband by her own uninhibited enjoyment. She reveled in loss of control and a selfish celebration of her feelings.

There were temporary relapses, but from that time on the sexual part of their marriage took a turn for the better. Jenny realized that focusing on her orgasm and enjoying her own feelings might seem selfish, but it was also a turn-on. In a paradoxical way, she found she gained so much better control of her love life as she was able to let go of control.

FIVE CHARACTER TRAITS OF A GREAT LOVER

We often forget that sex, in God's plan, is *not what we do to somebody,* but is *who we are.* It is not just great technique, but is rather a *relationship; the level of enjoyment is directly proportional to the person we have become.* We can learn all the right moves and become an expert technical lover, but if we are not loving, playful, honest, disciplined, and creatively romantic, our lovemaking will fizzle.

People often ask me, "Why is our sex life in such a rut? Why is our lovemaking having such diminishing returns?" I first check on whether they are in a committed, loving relationship, or are they only out for physical satisfaction. Then I explore whether they have ever taken the time to develop the necessary personality traits of great lovers.

1. Playfulness. Can you be playful? Perhaps you are wondering just what playfulness is. It is the ability to let go of control and to frolic and be silly. It is feeling you deserve to have fun and being able to anticipate it, then enjoying it as you create it. A child can get excited for a whole day about an anticipated ice cream cone, but adults have to be on their vacation two days before they relax. Playfulness is perhaps best described in childlike terms of feeling excited and curious, eager, and easily emotional. It is the ability to be spontaneous with enthusiasm and laughter.

Dee struggled with being playful. Then she started observing children and learning their traits. Jordan helped as they learned to trust each other. He could clown around more easily and was able to model playfulness for her. She found it difficult to relax her intensity, but she practiced being spontaneous and gradually grew less self-conscious. She unleashed her curiosity and explored new feelings and behaviors. It was difficult, but she learned to play at sex, and the playfulness spilled over into all areas of her life.

2. Love. There are so many facets to this character trait. A most important one is loving yourself and enjoying/accepting the body God gave you. Self-esteem and a good body image are a part of healthy self-love and being a great lover. Think how hard it is to reach out and focus on someone else when you feel bad about yourself. Love is also the respect and unconditional acceptance of another person; it is the ability to care for and nurture your mate. Love is gentle and kind and forgiving as you build intimate companionship.

Couples are often surprised how quickly their sex life deteriorates when love is lost in conflict and hatred. This is a powerful testimony to sex reflecting the whole relationship. So often wives, who are better at involving feelings and romance in their sexuality, state they would feel so much more sexually aroused if there were more loving gestures—help with household duties and nonsexual affection—caresses and hugs. Both mates need to lovingly build a reservoir of empathetic knowledge about their partner's needs and enjoyment. You want greater sexual frequency? Truly learn to love and give pleasure to each other!

3. *Honesty.* Sexual games and dishonesty are great sabotages and easy to fall into. Joe took awhile owning up to how boring sex had become with Gwynn. When they finally had an assertive confrontation of the issue, she too confessed how routine things had become; though she wasn't faking orgasms, she sure was having to stretch it to show any excitement or passion. They did the smart thing as they set aside time for open discussion when they were rested and fully clothed. So many couples start sniping or making suggestions during loveplay and both end up on the bedpost, hurt and angry.

Gwynn was upset because she could not refuse sex or make a suggestion without Joe getting hurt and pouting. She also felt an honest relationship involved his trusting her that she enjoyed sex and would initiate it if he gave her a chance. That set Joe off and he stated he got angry when he played all the initiating games and rituals like a quick shower and rubbing her back, only to get turned down. If he came right out and asked for sexual activity, she told him that was all he ever thought about and couldn't he be more romantic in his approaches.

It was a great air-clearing, honest discussion, and confrontation. Gwynn took the courage to look into herself and realize she gave conflicting messages; she also tried to tell Joe the general flavor and approaches of initiating that would work best with her. Joe stated he would feel better and reassured of her interest if she would set another time to make love if she had to refuse on a given night. They talked about techniques and variety and were more honest than they had been in years. Joe finally heard Gwynn when she said she did not need an orgasm every time. Gwynn better understood Joe's fears when he felt she put sex on the back burner. Both were pleased with the positive changes that took place as they openly communicated their sexual needs and engaged in honest dialogue.

4. *Romantic creativity.* Good sexual lovers are people who have taken the time to unfold their romantic creativity. Every person has an exciting romantic side, but few take the time and energy to develop it. I am amazed how couples come through in imaginative ways when I tell them their sex life is in a rut and I want them to plan in a sexy surprise for their mate this week. Everyone can learn the importance of sensuality and setting the mood, as ambiance is enhanced and anticipation builds.

As Joe and Gwynn started opening up, they took the time to individually list things they found special, romantic, or sexually arousing. They both discovered that many of the items on their list, from a surprise gift to lingerie to foot-and-leg massage to showers together, were all things they both enjoyed. They instituted romantic dinners with candlelight and soft, sexy glances. They unleashed their romantic creativity and enjoyed the increased excitement with a warm give-and-take. It got to be a game between them as they developed the romantic part of their personalities in creative ways.

5. *Discipline.* This may seem an odd character trait to include for a lover, and the opposite of spontaneous, playful, or creative. We have already discussed the lack of structure and priority. Undisciplined mates will end up with very infrequent sex. They may also have low commitment to the marriage and think the grass is greener elsewhere.

Norm found discipline very important as he rebuilt his

marriage and sex life after his affair. He had let his actions, and especially his thought life, become very undisciplined. He constantly tuned into every sexual cue in his environment and ran with it, mentally undressing other women. As he tuned back to Sandi and patiently postponed immediate pleasure for long-term satisfaction, he started appreciating sexuality in a refreshingly new way. He took the time and energy to be romantic and enrich his sex life with his wife. The loving, relational sex became so much more rewarding than undisciplined fantasy and illicit liasons.

Norm discovered the crucial nature of being a disciplined person in order to be a great sexual lover. He planned frequency as he set limits and kept out adulterating elements. He also patiently developed better skills and attitudes and carefully nurtured those crucial components of sexual intimacy—commitment and companionship.

SEVEN ENJOYABLE WAYS TO REVIVE PASSION

There is no magical Venus Butterfly technique that will instantly revitalize your lovemaking. But of all people, Christian couples should be loving, playful, creative, and open to ways to enhance God's special gift of sexuality. The following ideas are springboards for your own imagination and initiative.

1. Natural aphrodisiacs. Many couples wish for a magical love potion and neglect the many natural ways to enhance their sex life. I hear this story so often, "We had the best sex on vacation; we left the kids with their grandmother and we did it more in ten days than we have in the past three months." I have pondered this phenomenon and have come up with four great aphrodisiacs:

— being rested rather than tired
— uninterrupted time free from stress and distractions
— time alone to play together and bond
— the adventure of a hotel or having sex in the middle of the day.

The components of a vacation are great natural aphrodisiacs and are available without a whole week away. A good night's rest, a quick nap Sunday afternoon, or starting at 9 P.M. versus 11:30, can do wonders for the lovemaking that follows. Putting a lock on the door or creating two uninterrupted hours on a Saturday night, with the chores all done and a romantic dinner preceding, can make for exciting sex.

I often tell couples that the fun of their sex life will be in direct proportion to the time they spend alone together as companions. Great relational sex is based on comfortable togetherness and enjoyable bonding. This doesn't come just in the bedroom but while walking the beach, shopping, or eating together. My wife and I have started doing twenty-four-hour weekends away. We will leave Friday or Saturday night, stay at a bed and breakfast or hotel, and come back the next day. This is amazingly restorative to our relationship and our sex life.

I am not sure what it is about risk or adventure that is sexually arousing. Perhaps it is a human need for excitement or variety. There are ways to meet this need without having an affair or some equally destructive behavior. Vacations provide some element of doing the forbidden or unusual, like sex in the afternoon or a quickie in a secluded cove. Hotels give some of that feeling as you are away from the home environment. Couples can create the sense of excitement at home too by having sex in a room other than the bedroom or skinny-dipping in the pool or standing nude in a rainstorm (sans lightning, of course). There are many natural aphrodisiacs we seldom employ.

2. Sexual surprises. Every couple should try to plan a sexual surprise for each other at least once a month. My favorite example is the couple in which the wife was complaining about his busy schedule and lack of sexual frequency. It was December and one night while she was out jogging, he arranged a mattress by the Christmas tree and met her at the front door in the buff with only a candle in his hand and the Christmas lights twinkling in the background. They were still grinning two days later when they came in for their counseling session.

I have never met an individual who couldn't arrange creative surprises, everything from costume to place to creating a fantasy to arousing curiosity and anticipation. A surprise is making something unexpected happen, and there is a myriad of unexpected events an imaginative couple can arrange.

3. Sensual focusing. God gave us our senses—touch, smell, hearing, taste, sight—and an ability to be sensuous. You can enhance your sex life by focusing on all your senses, not only touch. Take a shower together and gently soap each other. Sleep nude and hug. Plan romantic dinners and enjoy the sensuality of fine food and soft lighting as you revel in each other's companionship. Give flowers and candy; play soft or pulsing music; rub warm oil on dry skin. Are you using all of your senses?

The following exercise is called *Sensate Focus* and was first developed by the sex therapists Masters and Johnson to help couples tune back into their sensuality and sexuality. Block out thirty minutes of relaxed, uninterrupted time. Take off clothing and one partner start off as giver and the other the receiver. For fifteen minutes the giver can stroke and caress the receiver's body, front and back but excluding genital areas and breasts. This is for your own pleasure and there are no performance standards, just the sensual enjoyment of your mate's body, as you focus on feelings with a relaxed appreciation of sensuality. Now switch roles and repeat over the last fifteen minutes. Don't proceed to intercourse. Find a renewed understanding and valuing of being sensual.

4. Sex talk. Do you say anything while you are making love? Do you comment on what you would like or enjoy? "Wow, that's great." "A little faster." With one couple I was counseling, the wife wished her husband weren't so silent during lovemaking. I kidded him and said maybe we should practice groaning here in the office. He blushed and refused. We then discussed verbal and nonverbal ways to help sexual arousal and enjoyment. The next session I asked him if he had groaned and if she had noticed. He replied, "Yes, I immediately pointed it out," and they both laughed. The playfulness and communication were definitely increasing. Discuss with your mate how you could increase verbal and nonverbal communication to enhance excitement and pleasure.

Do you ever discuss things you might like to include in your lovemaking? Sex therapist Sandra Leiblum suggests an interesting exercise called Sexual Scripting that every couple should try. Each of you write down in a brief way the script of your normal lovemaking session. Do this from your point of view, with your observations on what you normally do: activity, arousal, and enjoyment. Now each of you write up your ideal script of how you would program your sexual activity for maximum pleasure. Block out at least an uninterrupted hour and together go over both of your scripts.[1]

Did you have different views of what actually happens? Does the ideal script of your mate surprise you? What might you wish to incorporate into your lovemaking?

Couples can greatly enhance their sex lives by talking more, both in bed and also outside the bedroom. So many couples talk about every area of their marriage but are reluctant to have frank, sexual conversations. Here are two exercises that may get you started. Take advantage of this inexpensive but effective aphrodisiac: talking sexually!

● TIME OUT_____

1. What animal would best describe you as a sexual person? What color? What kind of car? Which Olympic sport? Relate both where you are now and what you would like to be.
2. They are making a movie of your love life. What would be its title? The theme song? Type of movie? Length? Which actor and actress would play your parts? Now do these same questions with your ideal sexual script.

---

5. *Invest in your sex life.* Pretend you and your mate have just been given $100,000 to invest in enriching your sex life. How would you spend it? A great way to revive the passion in your relationship is to budget some money to strategically boost your sex life. What do you need to spend this year?

Have you been neglecting vacations? Do you need a second honeymoon? Do you spend enough on baby-sitters and getting out alone together two or three times a month? Have you been promising to go get some counseling and work

1. Sandra Leiblum, *Sexual Desire Disorders*. New York: The Guilford Press, 1988, p. 168.

through an area that keeps sabotaging your love life? Do you need a bed that doesn't squeak? A more private door? Drapes? New lingerie? Some household help to preserve energy? Sit down and discuss with your partner how the two of you could invest in your sex life and revitalize that part of your relationship.

6. Be different! This sexual enhancer is tied into the needed character trait of being romantically creative. A growing, vital sex life stays out of ruts; the way to do this creatively is to be different. This is not to say there aren't certain positions, ways of caressing, rhythms, and movements that are favorites and will be used in a comfortable, enjoyable way time and again. But even these may grow old.

As Joe and Gwynn were developing the creatively romantic side of their personalities, they decided that at least once on the weekend they would try to be different. It became a game. If they usually made love in the bedroom, they tried the living room. They loosed their childlike curiosity and experimentation as they tried new positions and making love with their clothes on, excluding intercourse, only intercourse. They read books and bought props like big pillows and a shower massage. They followed the advice of Cliff and Joyce Penner who encourage, "Whatever variation you use — however crazy it might seem — if it creates fun and laughter and does not have to lead to intercourse, you have a good start on keeping alive your total sexual expression with each other."[2] "Different" became Joe and Gwynn's operative word and truly revolutionized their sex life. Remember, *creativity* starts with who you are and spills over into what you do.

7. Do it! I have a prescription which, if followed, will guarantee your sex life will never be the same. *Make love every day for ten days in a row!* Start on Friday and have sexual activity every day through to the following Sunday. You will learn many valuable lessons that will help you resurrect passion and dramatically change your personal and relational sexuality.

You will learn important lessons about structuring time to make sex a priority. You will be forced into variety with

---

2. Cliff and Joyce Penner, *The Gift of Sex: A Christian Guide to Sexual Fulfillment.* Waco, Texas: Word, Inc. 1981, p. 117.

increased frequency, and sex will grow comfortable and expected, rather than awkward or unusual. You will bond in a way that grabbing a few minutes of conversation or a hurried meal together would never do. Probably this will be the most excitement you have ever packed into ten days. Things will never be the same.

This is a valuable prescription because there is no substitute for time and frequency. You will have a better sex life if you spend forty-five minutes a session rather than fifteen. With love, honesty, and creativity, you are more likely to have a passionate love life making love four times a week rather than twice a month. It is sound advice to say, "Do it!" as a great method for reviving passion and pleasure. The wise lover also realizes doing it includes so much more than intercourse and orgasm.

There are no magical answers to enhancing your sex life. But if you and your partner are willing to overcome the common sabotages, build the necessary character traits, and try the preceding seven ideas for recapturing and increasing passion, you can better enjoy God's good gift of sexuality.

For Further Reading

Cliff and Joyce Penner, *The Gift of Sex: A Christian Guide to Sexual Fulfillment*. Waco, Texas: Word, Inc., 1981.

Ed and Gaye Wheat, *Intended for Pleasure*. Old Tappan, New Jersey: Fleming H. Revell Company, 1977.

Dagmar O'Connor, *How to Make Love to the Same Person for the Rest of Your Life and Still Love It*. New York: Bantam Books, 1985.

CHAPTER THIRTEEN

Building Your Support Network

✠

A solid support network enhances and guards great intimacy. A best friend knows us well enough to keep us on our toes, a baby-sitter allows us time to be alone together, a challenging minister pushes us to grow spiritually, and Mom encourages us to take vacations. I often wonder, as I look at my own marriage and those of others, why we neglect so vital a component for encouraging companionship.

Norm had a best friend in Bob, but at times they failed to keep in contact to use each other for accountability. Jenny struggled because in her perfectionism she would not lean on her network, since she did not trust them to do as good a job as she could. Jerry and Lisa were fairly new in their neighborhood and were uncertain how to mobilize an adequate baby-sitting network. Tom longed for a best friend, like Evie was for his wife, Laura. He was not sure how to make and maintain close friendships.

This chapter examines the types of support a functioning marriage utilizes. Some of these areas may trigger needs in your own relationship. The rest of the chapter discusses some of the sabotages, and then the skills needed to mobilize and manage your support system better.

AREAS OF YOUR SUPPORT NETWORK

There are seven common support areas couples can look to for assistance in maintaining intimate companionship. Think through your marriage carefully to pinpoint places where you and your mate may need to do some work.

● TIMESAVERS. There are people, services, and machines that can free up time for us to use in more strategic ways. My wife wanted a flower bed put in and I promised for months that I would get to it. She finally paid a handyman to do it and it was the best thirty dollars we spent that month. The most needed and common problem for parents is baby-sitting. I have come to realize that a good baby-sitter is sometimes more therapeutic than a therapist, as mates take time to be alone together. Barter for services, create a baby-sitting co-op where you share with other parents, seek out teens who are too young to do other work, find grandparents or godparents who want to be with children now and again, or a Mother's Morning Out program. Remember to keep creative and persistent with the timesavers. Jerry and Lisa persisted until they created an adequate baby-sitting network. Don't fall into the perfectionist or penny-pinching habit of doing everything yourself. Purchase or barter for services so you can allocate time for self and intimacy. It may be baby-sitters, a maid once a week to do bathrooms and vacuuming, or someone to clean gutters and rake leaves.

● **TIME OUT** _____

1. Without thought of cost or availability, brainstorm with your mate on what timesavers would really help your marriage.
2. Negotiate and problem-solve with your mate around budget and feasibility; stretch a little and work together to institute one change in the timesaver area of your relationship.

_____

● FRIENDSHIP. This area can make or break an intimate companionship. Evaluate your friendship network by regarding it as a continuum from casual to intimate.

casual   close   intimate

We need different kinds of friends along this line. There are neighbors we would consider casual friends, who keep an eye on our house and pick up our mail and newspapers when we are out of town. Other casual friends may be tennis buddies or aerobics partners, a financial adviser, an usher at church, or a business associate.

My close friends know my life well and are aware enough to pray for specific requests and concerns. There is self-disclosure and I lean on them. I also value my colleagues at the counseling center. In a closer manner, I share personal and professional things and invite their comment. I expect them to hold me accountable to God's economy. We have parties and do things socially together. I also attend a Bible study every Thursday morning. The men in the group have been very interested and supportive of my efforts with this book and of other personal areas of my life. A couple of these men have moved on the continuum to be closer to the intimate side of the scale, as I share my temptations and successes and get needed feedback.

In the close-to-intimate area are also several couples who do things regularly with my wife and me. They know much of our past and present and we trust them. When with them we feel unconditional acceptance. Cathy and I have both said how enriching it is to our marriage to be around other couple friends who are also building intimate companionship. I have some long distance friends who used to be intimate with me and I still regard as close. They fill a needed role as a sympathetic listening ear or to be happy with me over a victory. We need such people in our lives.

The difference between a close and intimate friend is in part the availability of that person and the time and energy invested in the relationship. Intimate friends truly know and accept us as we share contact weekly or daily with them. Laura deeply enjoyed and relied on her friend Evie. She did not keep any secrets from her and counted on her to be a confidential sounding board. She realized there were some secrets it was best to share with an intimate friend like Evie, who could be more detached than her husband, Tom.

She remembered one dangerous male relationship Evie rescued her from. Laura had had good male friendships but she thought now that a same-sex best friend was more prudent. Evie seemed to understand her female reality better—and no matter how hard you tried, with a male friend there often are sexual feelings to fog the relationship.

Couples plagued by the intimacy dragons need to restore their mates as intimate friends. Your spouse should be not only your best friend, but also your intimate companion and an important part of your support network. Like any intimate friend, your spouse should build your self-esteem and help you become the best possible person—by complimenting, confronting, and loving.

● TIME OUT_____

1. What part of the friendship continuum (casual, close, intimate) do you need to improve? Why do you think you are weak in that area and what could you begin to do this week to improve that part of your network?
2. How many intimate friends would you desire and be able to handle at one time? Which of your close friends might you consider moving into the intimate category? What two things could you do to increase intimacy? (ask for help in something, share an activity, risk revealing some private area of your life, etc.)

_____

● PROFESSIONAL SERVICES. This part of your support network may not seem to have a direct impact on your intimate companionship. But hasn't a good plumber or caterer helped your marriage at some time? Do you currently have a competent electrician, dentist, tailor, pediatrician, car mechanic, lawyer, heating and air conditioning service, accountant, decorator, doctor, and clothes consultant?

Holes in this part of the network can create lots of problems. Jenny grew up with a dad who was a real handyman. He hung wallpaper, fixed the toilet, put in a dimmer switch, and replaced the wood in the front porch. Alex struggled to assemble the children's swingset, even though it had detailed directions and a wrench included. They had many fights until one day Jenny's best friend, Sharon, told her to grow up and quit expecting Alex to duplicate her dad. She said she wished Jenny would quit griping and moaning, and find the professional help she needed.

Sharon had some personal investment in her advice. She and her husband, Jack, had gone round and round because she was not as domestic as his mother. She couldn't sew, did not have an eye for decorating, and was an average cook. Their marriage improved when he quit nitpicking, they found a good tailor, paid a decorator for advice, and went out to eat when he craved food with fancy sauces.

Another common problem is the husband or wife who is capable of doing professional tasks (putting a fan in the ceiling, hemming pants, changing the car gasket, painting a room, doing taxes) but never gets them done. Such people intend well; they feel guilt as the chores hang over their heads, and their mates stay frustrated. Like the timesavers, professional services are a strategic point for enhancing intimacy.

If this seems commonsense advice, then just do it! People come to me seeking deep answers to their depression and insomnia. I ask them about their last medical checkup, their exercise, and diet. Health and its side effects have a tremendous impact on intimacy. Consulting a health professional may be what you need as much as better communication skills.

● TIME OUT

1. When has professional help saved your neck and helped your intimacy along? What professional task can you do but you would rather not take the time for?
2. Brainstorm with your mate and strategically use one professional this month to augment your relationship.

● GROWTH ASSOCIATES. When Tom and Laura rescued their marriage from the dragon of codependent craziness, they worked very hard to develop a network that could both teach and encourage them in their changes. They especially appreciated their minister who fit the biblical idea of a shepherd — guiding, correcting, and loving them into change. Their couples Sunday School class was also a real boost, since the members were open and real in sharing their struggles. They did not feel alone or abnormal when so many people confessed the same rough edges and were together encouraging each other to grow.

Their marriage counselor coached them on a variety of needed skills as he carefully helped them heal their scars and strike a blow at ineptness. Tom especially was surprised at how much he had taken for granted in his lack of understanding about intimacy. As he grew, he got excited about the potential for a great relationship. He and Laura were able to attend several skill-building workshops, and a marriage enrichment weekend was a special time of rebonding. The couple who led it had been through so much and were a great inspiration. They decided to attend a strategic couples seminar at least once a year and to go back to their marriage counselor every six months for a tune-up.

Tom signed up for a Twelve-Step codependency group to work through some of his childhood scars. He found this very enlightening, painful, and supportive. Laura joined a women's Bible study which offered encouragement and some practical advice on relationships and parenting. They each worked on their spiritual and emotional journey, drawing closer to God and each other.

As a part of their growth process, Laura went back to college to pursue the degree she had always longed for. It was time consuming but important. Tom occasionally was able to benefit from some spin-off advantages, like the creative writing seminar they attended together. Both increased in self-confidence and peacefulness as they worked on improving the growth network they had created, utilizing it to the maximum.

● TIME OUT

1. Where are you personally stagnant and in need of strengthening your growth network? How about relationally? What is keeping you from getting some counseling? Joining a class?
2. Everyone needs to be on a spiritual journey with a rela-

tionship to God. What would encourage you in this process: a church fellowship, a shepherd, a study group,
more prayer and meditation?

● FAMILY. Will sat in my office and bluntly asked if he
had to have a relationship with his dad. He appreciated what
his mom meant in his life as she loved the grandkids and had
come to help Carrie for a week after each baby was born. He
enjoyed a special relationship with his brother and loved his
uncle and aunt who had kept him a couple weeks each
summer as he was growing up. But his dad had left when he
was eight and could still be very angry and coldly distant.

Will was asking a tough question; family is a great part of
a support network. Do we have to maintain a relationship
with everyone, especially if they choose not to be involved or
supportive? I don't think so. Stored up anger and resentment
needs to be worked through, or it can become a cancer that
consumes much emotional energy. But as with other parts of
our network, we have to develop our family relationships
honestly and strategically. Some grandparents feel imposed
on by baby-sitting duties and that is okay. Some family members have their own issues and problems and may never be
there for us.

Will's sister had four children and was content to build her
life around them. She and his brother-in-law were gracious
when Will visited them, but they never extended themselves.
Will's brother, on the other hand, called frequently and the
two families vacationed together. They enjoyed a warm, supportive friendship. Will and Carrie felt freedom as they let go
of guilt and enjoyed developing the family relationships and
support which were possible. At a family reunion recently,
they met two cousins they had not seen in years. They found
they had a lot in common with them and decided to cultivate
a closer relationship with them over the coming year.

● TIME OUT _____

1. With which family members would you like to cultivate
   better supportive relationships? With which members do

you need to consider the obstacles and relax your efforts?
2. There is at least one member of your immediate or extended family you have not cultivated a relationship with, but would enjoy if you did. Who is it and how could you do that?

● LEISURE NETWORK. Some mental health hospitals see such an importance in this area of a person's life that they have a full-time staff person who is leisure time coordinator. Leisure activities, what we do to relax and recreate, can vary widely. Here is a sampling of possible resources as you build your network: Join a tennis or volleyball team, go backpacking or canoeing, participate in an acting class, take art lessons, create your own "diners club" with three or four other couples and once a month eat at someone's house, find friends who like ethnic restaurants or classic movies, buy season tickets to a concert series and take a new couple each time.

The possibilities are as wide as your interests and creativity. Try to include in your network some new activities. I think of my colleagues Bill and Linda Buchanan who just returned from backpacking in Colorado for a week. This was a spontaneous venture for trying something new. Include both individual and joint forms of relaxing and recreating. The marriage dragons and stress have a dampening effect on leisure time, relaxation, and enjoyment. Unfortunately, just when the dragons attack is the time couples need leisure stress-reducers the most.

● TIME OUT ———————————————

1. Think through five things you enjoy doing individually with your leisure time and five things you would like to do as a couple. Make up another list guessing what your mate would put down. Compare and discuss.
2. Many couples say they have nothing in common in leisure activities. This is seldom true, but it may take some creativity to come up with new activities and then persistence in learning to like them. What are five things you would

agree to try as a couple? Select two of them and set realistic plans for following through.

● YOUR PARTNER. We mentioned mates under the area of intimate friendships, but they deserve a special category in your support network. Your mate is your partner in so many ways—encourager, confronter, business partner in establishing financial security, and companion. Catherine and I talk long hours over the directions we want to go. We are there to help each other clarify material values, spend wisely, and plan for the future. We are parental partners as we encourage and sort through our daughter's progress toward adulthood, and pray together for God's best in her life.

We do a variety of nurturing and mundane activities for each other. Cathy just got back from the cleaners and other errands, and I am about to embark on grocery shopping which she hates with a passion. She is a sergeant-at-arms in some areas of our life, like keeping a proper diet and sticking to the budget. I am motivator in terms of vacations and maintaining our cars. I also make sure we watch enough sports on television!

My wife meets so many needs, from the sexual to an affirming hug to being someone who will walk the mile and a half to Baskin-Robbins. We encourage each other to achieve individual dreams and to add new dimensions to our life and work. We are silent partners in each other's career, as we help the other fulfill personal and professional needs and goals. She knows I love to teach and she has supported me in this book, knowing it would open up opportunities. At times I help her hang heavy pictures or haul furniture, as she decorates homes in such a beautiful fashion.

● TIME OUT _____

1. How is your partnership? Sit knee-to-knee and complete the following sentences ten times each.
   a. "I appreciate when you . . ."
   b. "I wish we . . ."
2. Chapter 7 listed eight crucial areas in a marriage: finances,

sex, family, spirituality, career, companionship, support network, and leisure time. In which two of these do you wish you could achieve a better partnership and mutual support? Brainstorm on how it could be achieved.

SABOTAGES OF YOUR SUPPORT NETWORK

The couples who were attacked by the marriage dragons all sabotaged their support systems in different ways. Each could have been helped greatly in maintaining an intimate marriage, had they built and leaned more strategically on a network.

• UNDERUTILIZATION. As Norm got deeply involved in his runaway thought-life and adulterous behaviors, he avoided his friend Bob like the plague. Bob made him feel guilty and at this point in his life he did not want accountability or for anyone to confront his immature actions. Before Bob had gotten himself back on track, he had not been honest with Norm either. Neither availed himself of the help a best friend can be.

Jenny did not always trust her support network; in her perfectionism, she struggled with delegating tasks. She had a talented assistant who could sub for her with the handbell choir, but she was not able to let go and utilize her more often. Having a support network in place, whether a best friend, a competent substitute, a good physician, a loving pastor, or a tennis buddy, does no good if we avoid using them! It may be guilt, mistrust, fear of what the doctor might discover, or overbusyness; but regardless of the excuse, underutilization of our network hurts us and our intimacy.

• INADEQUATE DEVELOPMENT. Jerry and Lisa struggled with finding baby-sitters in a brand-new neighborhood. Tom was not sure how to create or be a best friend, but wanted to improve that area of his life. Their support networks had serious gaps, and they needed to shore up certain areas. But they were uncertain how to go about improving their network or finding needed resources.

Alex and Jenny were so busy and harassed that they could not find the time to create an adequate support network which would help them be less busy and harassed. Alex meant to find an accountant to help organize financial records and work on taxes, but he waited until the last minute and then had to do most of it himself. It was a vicious cycle.

Some people have character traits that contribute to the inadequacy of their support systems. Lisa was shy and this made it hard for her to be assertive and actively build her support and friendship networks.

• NEGLECT OF REVISIONS AND BACKUP. Laura got upset because her friend Evie was involved in her own struggles and wasn't there for her when she needed to talk. Tom found he had to make an appointment two weeks in advance to see his minister for pastoral counseling. By that time the immediate need had passed. Both discovered that a support system is not static but needs constant revisions. People may move, get too involved, or become otherwise unavailable.

Tom and Laura were finally able to expand their network and make provisions for a backup plan. Yet, they felt angry and thought about writing off the people who had not had time. Laura valued Evie as a friend though, and knew in time she would be more available. The next time Evie or the pastor came through, they were happy they had not acted rashly and cut off their nose to spite their face. They eventually recognized that life and support systems are always changing and that they had to be flexible.

• BEING PART OF THE PROBLEM. As Nancy was increasingly turned off by Bruce and they drifted further apart, she began spending more time with friends and in church activities to avoid intimacy at home. She got involved with many committees and started hanging out with her best friend, Karyn. Karyn was going through a divorce and did not know how Nancy could stay with Bruce when he was such a jerk. Nancy's support network became an escape and hindrance, rather than a tool for growth and for building a better marriage.

Jenny discovered that sometimes when she leaned on others, her network was more of a liability than a help. Alex's mom meant well, but when she pitched in to help with a problem, Jenny spent more time taking care of Mom than receiving assistance. Last week by the time she had picked Mom up, gotten her prescription filled, arbitrated an argument Mom had with her neighbor, gotten her situated with the children and taken her home—the evening of baby-sitting seemed very dearly bought. Both Nancy and Jenny began making some strategic changes so their support network would be part of the solution rather than a problem.

MANAGING YOUR SUPPORT NETWORK

In building and utilizing your network, you need to watch for the common pitfalls just listed. Just having a support system is not enough; you need to avoid the sabotages that keep you from utilizing that network to strategically build intimacy and companionship. Here are five skills an individual or couple can employ to overcome sabotages and mobilize a great support network.

• BE A SMART CONSUMER. Wise consumers seek out the products that will most efficiently meet their needs. They learn how to shop and try to make decisions with their heads, not their hearts. It is important, in creating and strengthening a support network, to learn where and how to hunt for what you need. Tom sought friends in a support group and also at his church where he thought he could find spiritual and emotionally healthy men. He also learned better relational skills so he could carefully develop the relationships he desired.

Lisa originally found my name as a counselor through the Yellow Pages and then talked with me on the phone to ascertain whether counseling was appropriate and if I could give the assistance she needed. Will and Carrie decided certain family members were more hindrance than support, and sought out other relationships strategically. They gave up being duty-bound within their family. When his friend Norm was in the height of his craziness, Bob realized he needed another close friend. He sought out someone who could be there for him in a more consistent fashion than Norm was able to.

Alex and Jenny consulted their friends as well as Alex's colleagues and came up with three names of good accountants. They then interviewed them and chose the one best suited to their needs. Jerry helped Lisa reach out within the neighborhood to find baby-sitters; they met several delightful couples through their tennis organization with whom they could swap sitting time. Learn to use your consumer skills to mobilize your network.

• PSYCH YOURSELF UP. You probably won't have an adequate support network if you don't see the need for it. You have to see how something is going to help you before you are willing to make the changes to achieve it. After sweating over his taxes at the last minute, Alex launched out and found an accountant. Go back over in your mind each of the seven areas (timesavers, friendships, professional services, growth associates, family, leisure network, marital partner) and name a solid reason why each is vitally important. Psych yourself up to become a good consumer; mobilize a healthy self-interest.

Do you miss not having a best friend and a supportive sounding board? Can you visualize a romantic evening with your wife because you found a baby-sitter? Think what your marriage would be like if you and your mate could fight and resolve issues rather than wounding each other. A good support network has great pay-offs. As you visualize the pay-offs, make a phone call to someone who can be part of your support system.

• TACKLE THE IMPORTANT AREAS. The urgent often takes precedence over the important, and we never get to a vital task like building a better support network. As you psych yourself up and begin to follow through on your network, start with some small manageable steps. Pick two areas you strongly want to improve and take a beginning step in those two areas today. Remember a good objective/step is one that is behavioral, feasible, and scheduled. "Today I am going to call Sarah and see if she can have lunch with me Thursday or Friday." "I will take twenty minutes this evening to talk with Laura about who could stay with Stephanie, if we plan a long romantic weekend. I will call Laura right now so she can be thinking about it."

A friendship network provides an interesting and valuable service. Once you start talking about making a change, your friends won't let you forget it. A colleague will say, "Did you find that wallpaperer you were looking for?" Your mom will ask, "How is Weight Watchers going? Here are some fresh tomatoes." Start some manageable changes and you will find the process snowballs. As Jenny involved her assistant choir director, she had more time and energy to develop other needed areas of her support network. Tom took a fishing trip with a casual friend and learned so much about friendship that now several of his relationships are blossoming. Tackle some area today!

● ESTABLISH A ROUTINE. Part of managing a support network effectively is to decrease the busywork of mobilizing. After Laura began eating breakfast alone with Tom every Saturday morning, that time became sacred to them and they did not have to consult schedules to decide what to do on Saturday morning. Jenny's mom agreed to keep the children overnight once a month. Alex contracted for a heating and air conditioning service which every spring and fall made a house call and changed filters. Their phone number was also there for any emergencies. Establishing a routine eliminates time-consuming preparation work.

Anything that can become a habit and routine is also more likely to be maintained. It can also become a habit to not let an area of the support network be decimated so you have to start from scratch. Two close friends moving out of state should signal a need to fortify the friendship network. If your favorite baby-sitter starts to work at McDonald's, you have to find someone new. Build some routine into building and using your support network.

● CREATE SOME BACKUP. When Tom found his minister was not always available, he learned to also lean on an older Christian man in the church who enjoyed being his mentor and gave wise counsel. Jerry and Lisa created a whole network of baby-sitters so they wouldn't get stuck. Laura found several close friends who could stand in for Evie when she was unavailable. Alex located two good mechanics Jenny could call if the car broke down; this could compensate for his lack of skills and his busy work schedule. Now is the time to take action, sort through your seven areas and solicit some needed help!

CHAPTER FOURTEEN

The Journey of Becoming One-Flesh Companions

✠

God created the marvelous concept of marriage and intimate one-flesh companionship. "It is not good for the man to be alone. I will make a helper suitable for him. . . . For this reason a man will leave his father and mother and be united to his wife, and they will become one flesh. The man and his wife were both naked and they felt no shame" (Genesis 2:18-25). Talk about a great self-concept and unconditional love and acceptance! Adam and Eve could be totally naked physically and emotionally, with no hesitation or embarrassment. I envy them—becoming great companions is much tougher now than in the Garden of Eden.

COMPONENTS OF INTIMACY

Laura worried that if she stayed married she would lose her own identity and have to forfeit most of her personal goals. The concept of becoming one flesh with Tom, or anyone, was very unappealing. Marriage seemed a smothering institution to her.

Lisa struggled with being trapped in a union with a very unfulfilling man. As she tried to create a better companionship, her interpretation of biblical submission backfired as Jerry got more self-centered. *One flesh* became a synonym for frustration and loneliness, as their communication and connectedness broke down completely.

Each of the couples devastated by the marriage dragons

lost out on the true enjoyment and meaning of an intimate companionship. They all had misconceptions of what a one-flesh union really was, and needed to become students of intimacy and learn what God intended for marriage.

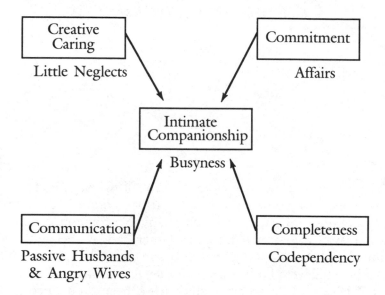

Companionship is at the heart of intimacy and, four components create and maintain that companionship. *Creative caring* or love energizes this union. *Commitment* protects and makes it special. *Communication* connects a couple and keeps the air clear. *Completeness* makes it possible for two whole people to form a healthy, fulfilling relationship. Certain marriage dragons are particularly lethal to these aspects of becoming one flesh. As the couples we met started to heal their marriages, they had to explore and work on understanding intimate companionship and then rebuilding its essential elements.

● COMPANIONSHIP. Companionship is the core goal of intimacy. Each of the couples whose relationships we explored wanted a warm, comfortable, vibrant togetherness. They desired this companionship in many different ways. They wanted a partner who was unconditionally on their side but would also confront their rough edges. They craved the mystery and excitement of sexual and emotional fulfillment and being playmates through life. Candlelight dinners, walks on the beach, and going to flea markets were all a part of creating history and traditions together.

Sometimes two separate items are fused together and the product is stronger than either of them separately. This is true of becoming one-flesh partners. I like the word *interdependence* to describe intimate companionship, because it refers to this fusion of selfishness and unselfishness. Becoming companions is a healthy blend of independence and dependence, of autonomy and submission.

Within intimate companionship, we can achieve more than we could alone or in tandem. We become the best individual we could be because we have a loving partner bringing out the finest in us and encouraging us to fully enjoy all our God-given strengths and abilities. We also build a wonderful dependence that allows us to rely on our mates, enjoy their nurturing, and look forward to time spent together. Such dependence is not clingy, smothering, or possessive because we also value uniqueness and encourage a healthy separateness. In an intimate marriage, we have the best of both worlds — this amazing God-designed synthesis with its interdependence of autonomy and submission — *a one-flesh partnership.*

The couples attacked by the intimacy dragons, but desiring God's wonderful companionship, realized that there were crucial aspects of intimacy they would have to strengthen. Their enjoyment of companionship depended on their improving four supportive components: Commitment — Creative Caring — Communication — Completeness.

Jerry and Lisa worked on all four areas as they nurtured their love with caring behaviors and the feelings slowly returned. They shored up their commitment to each other and protected their relationship by making better choices. Both, especially Jerry, worked hard to get better relational skills and to live more comfortably with incompatibility. They became better at recognizing and changing their codependency and rough edges which detracted. Lisa was pleased that as they improved the other components of intimacy, their companionship became closer and more meaningful. Their love-making increased and became more satisfying.

Nancy and Bruce went from a solid partnership and warm companionship into a nitpicking separateness. As they started to rebuild their relationship, they came to appreciate another important dynamic of intimate companionship: the wounds received from a destructive relationship can be healed best by moving through the same experiences, but now in a positive and loving relationship. They were gun-shy at first, but with love and greater skillfullness they relived old, hurtful incidents. They dealt with misunderstandings around the miscarriage and Nancy's need for respect and empathy. This time there was healing as they were honest and thorough, not neglecting to immediately deal with any hurt feelings. They slowly rebuilt trust and love through their renewed relationship.

Bruce discussed this concept with his friend Clark who had remarried. Clark confirmed that he too had experienced the necessary and wonderful healing of an intimate companionship. Traumatic events like angry vacation scenes had slowly been erased as he and Ingrid enjoyed smooth vacations and affirming interactions. He felt loved and like a great lover once again, as he healed old scars through new positive experiences with Ingrid.

The couples discovered that meaningful companionship was often in proportion to the time and experiences they shared. They set goals and priorities with each other for their relationship. They learned to like each other and value the comfortable harbor they were creating. They saved up events to share and couldn't wait to disclose some exciting personal victory. They always kept an eye on creative caring, commitment, communication, and completeness—knowing how important these were in creating and maintaining intimacy.

● TIME OUT_____

1. What personal scars do you need to discuss with your mate as you plan activities together that can help you heal? How will you work through feeling abandoned, a poor body image, the fear of conflict, etc.?
2. Assume you need two more hours a week of quality time with your mate. Where will you find these two hours?

● CREATIVE CARING. Nancy ceased to love Bruce as their intimacy slowly succumbed to an onslaught of nitpicking and neglect. What exactly does it mean when we cease to love someone? Often I will have couples state, "I love my mate very much — I just don't like her at all right now." Sometimes it is, "I have fallen in love with someone else," or "I love him but we are like roommates — we aren't lovers anymore."

A pretty young woman told me she was in an almost perfect dating relationship, but was about to break up with the guy. She explained that he met all her nonnegotiables — he was a Christian, honest, had a good sense of humor, balanced his work and play, had an excellent job, and loved her. The hitch was that she was not in love with him; she felt no vibrations.

This made me think more deeply about the component of intimacy we call love or creative caring. Can we willfully produce or kill it? This young woman saw it more as a feeling, a combination of sexual attraction and warm, vibrant connectedness that she couldn't choose to create. Others see it as a deliberate act of the will to nurture someone and be committed to his or her spiritual well-being. This extends beyond the area of feelings and more into the realm of willpower and mental choices.

Creative caring can bring such joy to companionship that it is no wonder we mourn its absence and seek to revive and deepen its energizing presence. But what exactly is it? A feeling? A choice? I think it can best be explained by examining three different Greek words for love: *eros, philia,* and *agape.*

1. Eros. The young lady who met her ideal man felt something was missing and was unable to connect on this important level. Often *eros* is simplistically passed off as sexual feelings or lust. The confused young lady, or the troubled man in my office after an affair, would disagree with such a simplistic definition. They would strongly state that this vital, complex component of love cannot be taken lightly. What is eros? It is sexual passion and fireworks; it is a strong attraction and crazy excitement; it is fusion and abandonment of our defensive walls; it is a rush and infatuation; it is getting lost in someone's eyes during romantic moments.

Couples will tell me, "We have outgrown those early, excited feelings and have become comfortable with each other." I always challenge this statement, because every marriage needs passion! I realize that long-term passion is built on companionable love (philia) and that romantic rushes will come and go, but we still need to be able to create second honeymoons.

While there are no magic formulas for heightening passionate feelings, there are some things that work. Because the basis of long-term excitement is *philia* and *agape,* we need to understand those concepts. I help the person coming to me after an extramarital affair to restore commitment (agape) and companionship (philia). Sexual passion and romantic feelings cannot blossom if we do not like or feel committed to a mate in sickness and in health. The willful choice to be loving (agape) assists the passionate feelings to grow.

We also need to recapture some of the fireworks and become infatuated with our mates on an ongoing basis. We can learn to cherish and focus on their strong points physically and personality-wise, forgetting expectations and letting go of other sexual fantasies. As one husband remarked, "She is such a cuddly, vibrant person that I forget the stretchmarks and ten extra pounds, as I revel in the texture of her skin and the excitement we experience just being together."

Make warm, romantic love as you put sex back in your marriage. Revive some passion by truly making time for each other.

Time together + Focused Sensuality = Greater Passion.

Quick sexual encounters seldom restore and deepen excitement and eros. Romantic dinners, weekends away from children and the house, trust and respect for each other, flowers and loving surprises, tuning in to sensuality and the joy of your partner, will definitely increase eros.

2. *Philia.* This Greek word for love presents the picture of a comfortable companionship. The wife who says, "I love him (agape commitment), but I just don't like him (philia) right now," is referring to this kind of love. When her hus-

band is being a jerk, she does not feel warm toward him or enjoy being with him, and she especially doesn't want sex. It is interesting how conflict or disgust turns off the eros, as well as much of the philia, in most women.

The companionable friendship of love usually develops after the initial eros has subsided into better perspective. It is made up of mutual interests, self-disclosing conversations, bonding experiences, and a comfortable togetherness. Philia is more interested in cooking an omelet together and propping our feet up than it is in having dinner at a fancy restaurant. As the marriage dragons strike, most couples experience some fallout in this area of their love.

It takes work to find mutually enjoyable activities and to devote *time, knowledge, and shared experiences* in order to grow closer. Joint ventures, a shoulder to cry on, sharing people and parties, learning some of our mate's language, nurturing in many little ways, all foster philia.

3. Agape. Pronounced a gáh pay, this aspect of love is based on choice and is unconditional. God loves His children this way; His love is not merited or based on how beautiful we are. As Bob was trying to get over his affair with Betty and restore his love for his wife, Jill, he grabbed hold of agape love. His feelings were strongly in Betty's favor, but he wanted his marriage to work and committed himself to that process. He renewed his vows and found the companionship improving week by week. The sexual attraction and passion took almost two years to recapture, but he found as he acted and chose to be loving, the philia and eros returned.

Agape was not "being in love" but "choosing to love" in a committed, self-sacrificing fashion. Both Jill and Bob struggled through tough times, but the joy and deep companionship they share today was worth the price of the journey. "Until death do us part" took on new meaning for them. Often they felt like giving up, but their wills and not their emotions carried them through, as they prayed for wisdom and courage. God blessed their efforts.

● TIME OUT _____

1. Discuss together which area of love (eros, philia, agape) the following activities would help the most: praying

together, a weekend away, a marriage seminar, learning tennis, having a child, putting a lock on the bedroom door, taking a cooking class, buying matching underwear.
2. Which area of love is most responsible for the feeling "in love"? What two things could you as a couple do this month to rekindle those passionate feelings?

● COMMITMENT. This aspect of intimacy is a *process* composed of a *series of choices* to create an exclusive relationship with our mate. Some of our choices are highly visible stakes we have driven in the ground, altars we have created as special and easily remembered symbols of our commitment. The wedding vows are one of these symbols, similar to the pillar Jacob erected in Bethel to serve as a reminder of God's promise and blessing (Genesis 28:18). It helps to remember these formal choices we have made and had others witness with us—our marriage covenant, our home mortgage note, that special anniversary, a child's birth certificate. In commitment, a couple is declaring to each other, "Out of all the people in the world, I have chosen you to be in a special, loving companionship."

Norm, Alex, and so many others can testify that it is not only the large choices but also the little unwitnessed ones that can make a great difference. Norm had neglected a whole series of little choices that would have affirmed his commitment to Sandi, before he ended up in bed with Alison. He did not choose to make time for Sandi but spent increasing time with friends at Qunicy's Pub and commiserating on the phone about Alison's bad marriage. He did not choose to discipline his thought life but let his fantasies run wild concerning Kim, the cute Spanish teacher. He did not choose to confront little dissatisfactions with Sandi, but nitpicked as he developed a serious case of negativity. With hindsight, Norm could pick out the many poor choices and the disintegration of his committed intimacy over the course of six months.

Alex remembered choosing to work late on a night Jenny desperately needed him at home. He chose not to say no to a new ministry at church, though he knew he was already running on empty. He avoided sex because of fatigue and irritability. Like Norm, he made a series of choices that pushed his mate away. He had to learn the hard way that intimacy can flourish only if a couple spends quality time alone together. Alex and Jenny renewed their commitment to reserve time and energy for each other. They started making better choices in various parts of their life and marriage.

These commitment choices to preserve and deepen intimacy often seem insignificant at the time because they pop up in all areas of marriage. It could mean calling off a lunch with a friend, deciding whether to have that third child, going on a weekend trip to a bed and breakfast, leaving work at the office, or buying that funny card and leaving it for her in her car. It can be going to a weekend communications seminar, apologizing for an unkind remark, or working harder to correct a personal character defect.

● TIME OUT

1. Slowly think over the eight key areas of your marriage: money, sex, family, spirituality, work and ministry, companionship, support network, and leisure time. Where have you been making some poor choices recently in preserving your one-flesh intimacy?
2. There is at least one thing you should do now to promote the special companionship of your marriage. Do it! The journey of 1,000 miles begins with the first step.

● COMMUNICATION. The process of making love is an excellent model for exploring the nature of intimate communication. Effective communication and great sex are a solid balance of healthy *attitudes* and a skillful understanding of *technique*. The attitudes are the starting point. A great lover is not simply someone who knows what to do in bed. The quality of lovemaking stems more from who the lover is than what he or she does.

Are you comfortable with sexuality? Do you enjoy your own body? Are you able to nurture and to be playful? Do you openly self-disclose needs and feelings? Do you create romance?

Intimate communication skills also begin with attitudes and they spill over into actions. Capable communicators are aware of their needs and feelings and able to assertively express them. They detach in a secure manner and truly empathize. They are comfortable with confrontation and conflict and are able to remain courteous as they seek to gather information and not go for the win. Enriching communication, whether sexual or nonsexual, connects mates together; it is built on a quality balance of attitudes and behaviors.

Though attitudes are the starting point, we should not diminish the importance of technique and behaviors. Good lovers know how to produce exciting feelings and bring them to a peak. Great communicators know how to stick to the topic, keep their voice down, and ask feedback questions.

Both intimate lovemaking and conversation are trying to create and share a bonding closeness. Both take risks and are nondefensively vulnerable as the partners are "naked and unashamed." Probably over ninety percent of our communication and lovemaking is nonverbal. Warmth, excitement, closeness is shared in an assertive, self-disclosing manner as soulmates grow close over time.

We must be careful not to rely solely on nonverbal communication. Mates can get lazy and start to assume or mindread. Messages need to be verbally communicated and feedback exchanged. I laugh to myself when a wife finally self-discloses to her husband, "I wish you wouldn't blow in my ear during lovemaking," and the husband quickly retorts, "I thought you loved that. Why didn't you say something two years ago?" She replies, "I liked it two years ago." People change and a continuing dialogue is irreplaceable.

● TIME OUT _____

1. How are you communicating in your lovemaking? Does it reflect your communication in general?
2. Why are you afraid of conflict? Do a quick review of chapter 10 and pick three communication principles you need to improve on. Simulate some situations and practice these skills with your mate.

• COMPLETENESS: Someone asked me recently what I would name as the most hurtful problem in marriage. I replied that it is incomplete and codependent mates. *It takes two whole people to put together meaningful intimacy.* We can rise only to the level of intimacy that our scars, our quirks, our codependent craziness allow.

The primary factor on this journey to completeness is a personal relationship to God, the Creator and Source of honesty, self-esteem, and sanity. As we allow Him into our lives through Christ and the Holy Spirit, the power of sinful destructiveness is broken. We are better able to understand and conform to His guidelines for great companionship.

In chapter 8 we looked at some of the ways we can heal codependent craziness and become complete. *Completeness* implies we have all the necessary parts for intimacy. Other people may be crucial to our personal completeness. Counseling or a growth group may prove invaluable. Involvement in a church fellowship and building a more effective friendship network can be healing. We can also use our mate to rub off the rough edges. A marriage is a tremendous lab experience for confrontation and change.

Progress toward deeper intimacy requires not only an increasing individual wholeness, but also a move toward couple wholeness. Tom and Laura fell into some tremendously destructive, codependent patterns. Their fights were very melodramatic but resolved nothing. They allowed each other's moods to dictate how they felt personally and both operated from many unrealistic expectations. Their relationship could vacillate from sexual closeness to angry defensiveness daily. Incompleteness reigned.

As Tom and Laura worked to decrease their individual insecurity and defensive walls, they began relating better. They also improved their communication skills and learned to assertively express their needs and feelings. As they acquired missing parts, they became more complete. A mutually satisfying friendship blossomed.

• TIME OUT

1. List three personal rough edges and discuss them in detail with your mate: where they came from, what triggers

them, how they sabotage, what could be done to change them.

2. Can you think of an example in your marriage of how some personal craziness contributed to a codependent relationship problem? You may find that even though you have gotten your individual acts together, the relational rough edges remain. Discuss through with your mate the destructive relational patterns you need to change.

ROADBLOCKS TO INTIMACY

On the journey toward intimate companionship, couples can get bogged down behind roadblocks. These barriers (Games, Walls, Stinking Thinking, Power Struggles) often involve the absence or distortion of *honesty, trust,* and *respect* — three qualities essential to achieving true intimacy.

● GAMES. As Norm moved deeper into his adulterous behaviors, he began playing dishonest games with himself and Sandi. He told outright lies and also rationalized to himself, "If my wife were more playful and interested in me, I would spend more time with her." In his blaming and denial, Norm would not accept his contributions to the problem, but put the responsibility on Sandi.

Couples can easily begin playing sexual games. Rather than dealing with their anger, they withhold sexual activity. Instead of honestly saying, "You hurt my feelings last night and I don't feel like making love this morning until we work on my anger," they mentally or perhaps subconsciously note, "No nookie for you for a while until you shape up."

Some mates get into destructive patterns that evolve from codependent craziness. Tom thought Laura was so insecure he could never meet her emotional needs. Therefore when she desired any affirmation, he blew up and withdrew. It was a crazy dance they developed with Tom avoiding and Laura pushing and both angry enough to kill. Games can seriously stymie companionship. Good communication, confrontational skills, and *rigorous honesty* have a way of overcoming this roadblock to intimacy.

● WALLS. In the course of living, each of us gets wounded and scarred, experiences deep disappointment, and feels abandoned. As a result, all of us build defensive walls to protect ourselves; the following exercise can help you see yours.

● TIME OUT

1. Visualize your wall. Imagine what it looks like. How tall is it? What is it made of? What are three pivotal factors that helped create the wall?
2. *What would someone have to do to get through your wall?* How would this help your intimacy?

Jill felt she would never be able to trust Bob—or any man. He had been so dishonest with his affairs and made a fool of her. Her dad had not been very dependable either and was never there for her in a consistent way. Her walls seemed higher than ever, and she wasn't sure her wounds would heal this time.

Bob wondered if he could ever redeem himself. He found though as he made changes, and built a track record of honesty and trustworthiness, that he slowly earned Jill's trust back. She dealt with some of the old feelings and unfinished business around her dad and chose willfully to let Bob back in. In a slow, scary process, she became more trusting and vulnerable. Jill felt better as she lowered her wall. The companionship became more fulfilling than it had ever been. It encouraged her to keep being open and take further risks.

● STINKING THINKING. I remember the couple who asked me to help them pick at each other's flaws and weak points. Their rationale was that if their marriage could survive that, it was truly meant to be. I assured them every mate had enough flaws—there is no Mr. or Mrs. Right—and that even the best of marriages could be destroyed, if flaws were constantly the primary focus. Nitpicking is a serious roadblock to intimacy. Do you remember the husband who chose to focus on his wife's strong points sexually, not her stretch marks or ten extra pounds? This positive mind-set created a great sex life.

Bruce and Nancy got caught up in stinking thinking as

their disrespect for each other grew. Bruce saw Nancy as a bossy, angry person and, sure enough, the more he focused on this, the more it became a self-fulfilling prophecy. Nancy's anger increased and she hated the marriage. Negativity killed any hope of companionship.

Laura struggled with another type of destructive thinking. She was skeptical of Tom ever changing as she hung on to past hurts. As she finally was able to let go and forgive, she was pleased to discover how much this helped Tom change. As she became more positive, Tom tried to live up to her confident expectations. They got on a positive roll and she was constantly affirmed by the way their friendship grew. She discovered that she had the power to choose the direction of their companionship.

● POWER STRUGGLES. In their first counseling session, Cory immediately brought up that Janie did not let him wear the pants in the family and contradicted him constantly. He wondered if she understood what submission was all about. I groaned to myself and realized that we were not dealing with submission but with a power struggle and a lack of trust and respect. Janie confirmed this as she angrily began her attack on Cory. Power struggles have a grand way of suffocating any hope of intimate companionship.

We began discussing better communication skills and the need to dialogue, not win. We also jumped into why they did not like and respect each other. Both Cory and Janie disagreed with me at first, but slowly acknowledged disappointed expectations and mistrust of their mate. Cory admitted fearing they might get too close because intimacy was sometimes scary. They both admitted being bullheaded and said that some of their fights had gotten very ugly. This destroyed their respect for each other and kept them distanced for days at a time.

With forgiveness, better relational skills, and a growing understanding and respect for each other, Cory and Janie lessened their need for control. They learned to compromise and practice flexibility. They started to trust that their partner was looking out for their best interests. They enjoyed this deeper level of intimacy as each refused to allow power struggles to develop.

INTIMATE BONDING

Bonding is a marvelous word and a most desirable element of intimacy. All of us living in God's wonderful economy of marriage realize that we have the opportunity for a very special companionship. We seek to maximize this potential with our mate — to be truly fulfilled, intimate, and bonded.

In one sense, intimate bonding is what this whole book is about: keeping the marriage dragons at bay so that we can negotiate this journey of becoming bonded soulmates.

Start by reviewing the common intimacy invaders and doing some preventive work.

1. Busyness. You can take for granted that you are too busy — it is an epidemic. What you choose to do about it will seriously affect the quality of intimacy you desire. Be courageous. You can make some changes — just do it!

2. Little neglects. Neglects are like a swarm of killer gnats. If you neglect the important little problems, they may grow into destructive mountains, and you may end up nitpicking your marriage to death. Neglect little loving gestures and love dies. Be honest. You're neglecting something in your marriage right now.

3. Affairs. Stay alert and humble. You are not immune to an extramarital affair. Set good boundaries so you do not get blindsided. Remember there are many things that can adulterate your marriage. You could name several that are potential hazards right now. Be careful.

4. Passive husbands, angry wives, and poor communication. Lack of relational skills is a real killer! Fortunately this problem is so correctable. Don't be overwhelmed; find a tutor and keep practicing.

5. Codependent craziness. We all are codependent to a degree and have some personal rough edges. We can also take for granted that our individual craziness has created some crazy marital patterns. Your companionship will only reach the level to which you have been able to get your individual and marital act together.

PRACTICE, PRACTICE, PRACTICE!

Remember that great bonding and a richer intimacy is based upon many commonsense relationship principles. As you incorporate these skills into your lifestyle, you will be amazed how intimate relating can gain momentum. The more you practice them, the more natural they become. As you read over a summary of the processes this book has developed, isn't it exciting how many of them you are already beginning to use?

1. Celebrate incompatibilities as you understand them and build a richness into your marriage.

2. Confess your sins to each other and experience acceptance and healing as the secrets are brought to the light of day.

3. Accept responsibility for your problems as each mate repents and works at making needed individual changes.

4. Learn to express those protective and healing emotions. Get angry, be jealous, envy some, and above all cry as you grieve over the loss and unfairness in life.

5. Tell your mate you are sorry, as you become humbly skillful at making amends.

6. Establish goals in your marriage and then build the structure for following through on them.

7. Know and love yourself; then enjoy your mate.

8. Mobilize a strong support network; you need other people for intimacy to blossom.

9. Make love for fun, for closeness, for nurturing, for excitement, for healing hurts, for procreation. God has given you a tremendous gift for enjoying intimacy in your sexuality.

10. Communication skills are part of the bottom line. I cannot say it more strongly: learn them or forever forfeit intimacy.

11. Above all, bring the Lord into your relationship and let Him help you conform to His economy.

The journey of becoming one flesh is exciting, fulfilling but hard work. Intimacy and a deeply satisfying companionship are achievable!

MAY GOD GRANT YOU WISDOM AND COURAGE.